Sibling teaching among the Agikuyu of Kenya

von

Maureen Mweru

Tectum Verlag
Marburg 2005

Coverabbildung: Copyright der Autorin

Mweru, Maureen:
Sibling teaching among the Agikuyu of Kenya
/ von Maureen Mweru
- Marburg : Tectum Verlag, 2005
Zugl.: Osnabrück, Univ. Diss. 2005
ISBN 978-3-8288-8810-4

© Tectum Verlag

Tectum Verlag
Marburg 2005

Acknowledgements

My profound gratitude goes to Prof. Dr. Heidi Keller for all her advice and without whom it would not have been possible to write this thesis. I am also sincerely grateful to Prof. Dr. Jürgen Kriz for all the helpful feedback he provided.

I cannot forget to thank my sponsors, the Katholischer Akademischer Ausländer Dienst (KAAD) for providing me with a scholarship that enabled me pursue my PhD studies in Germany and my gratitude also goes to Kenyatta University, Nairobi for granting me study leave.

I also wish to express my sincere gratitude to all the members of staff in the Department of Development and Culture, Faculty of Human Sciences, Osnabrück University for all the assistance they afforded me.

In addition, I also wish to express my sincere gratitude to my research assistant Teresia Wambui Kimuhu and her family for their hospitality and without whom the data collection phase of this study would not have been possible. I also owe special thanks to all the families in Gatundu North division of Thika district who participated in this study.

Last but not least I wish to thank my family in Kenya for absolutely everything.

TABLE OF CONTENTS

Acknowledgements 3
List of tables 7
List of figures and maps 9
List of photos 11

CHAPTER I: INTRODUCTION 13
1.1 Background of the study 13
1.2 Statement of the problem 14
1.3 Purpose of the Study 15

CHAPTER II: CONCEPTUAL FRAMEWORK 17
2.1 Intergenerational cultural transmission 17
2.2 Cultural learning and cultural teaching 21
2.2.1 Cultural learning 21
2.2.2 Cultural teaching 28
2.3 Sibling interaction 30
2.4 Play in a cultural perspective 34
2.5 The Agikuyu people 36
2.5.1 Children's socialization among the Agikuyu 37
2.6 Assumptions of the study 40

CHAPTER III: METHODOLOGY 43
3.1 Study site 43
3.1.1 Geographical location, topography and climate 43
3.1.2 Economic activities 44
3.1.3 District inhabitants and population 46
3.2 Time of study 46
3.3 Delimitations of the study 46
3.4 Sample frame 46
3.5 Participants 48
3.6 Instruments of the study 50
3.6.1 Video recording 50
3.6.2 Interview schedule 52
3.7 Teaching episodes 52
3.7.1 Variables used in quantitative analysis 53
3.7.1.1 Verbal discourse variables 53
3.7.1.2 Nonverbal discourse variables 54
3.7.1.3 Verbal, nonverbal discourse variables or both 57
3.7.1.4 Discourse variables as per assumptions of the study 63
3.8 Statistical analysis 64
3.9 Reliability 65

CHAPTER IV: RESULTS 67
4.1 Item analysis of the interview schedule 67
4.2 Statistical analysis of videotape data 70
4.2.1 Older siblings' support for the toddlers 70

4.2.2 Older siblings' manipulation of the toddlers 73
4.2.3 Older siblings' negative behaviour 75
4.2.4 Older siblings' use of verbal and nonverbal discourse variables 77
4.3 Qualitative data analysis of videotape data 79
4.4 Summary of the statistical and qualitative analysis 93

CHAPTER V: DISCUSSION 97
5.1 Variables of the study 97
5.1.1 Older siblings' support for the toddlers 97
5.1.2 Older siblings' manipulation of the toddlers 98
5.1.3 Older siblings' negative behaviour 99
5.2 General discussion 101

CHAPTER VI: CONCLUSION AND RECOMMENDATIONS 105
6.1 Conclusion 105
6.2 Recommendations 106
6.2.1 Parents 106
6.2.2 Educationalists 106
6.3 Future studies 107
6.4 Shortcomings and constraints of the study 108

References 111
Appendix 131
Curriculum Vitae 133

LIST OF TABLES

Table 1 Socio-demographic data of toddlers' parents 49

Table 2 Discourse variables as per study assumptions 63

Table 3 Individuals assisting in caretaking 67

Table 4 Toddlers mothers' views on meaning of teaching 68

Table 5 Toddlers mothers' views on when teaching should begin 69

Table 6 Toddlers mothers' reasons as to age when teaching should begin 71

LIST OF FIGURES AND MAPS

Figure 1	Location of Thika in Kenya	45
Figure 2	Means of descriptions and explanations by age group	72
Figure 3	Means of talk with demonstration by age group	72
Figure 4	Means of guiding toddlers' body by age group	73
Figure 5	Means of commands by age group	74
Figure 6	Means of feedback by age group	74
Figure 7	Means of verbal aggression by age group	75
Figure 8	Means of nonverbal aggression by age group	76
Figure 9	Means of verbal possessiveness by age group	76
Figure 10	Means of nonverbal possessiveness by age group	77
Figure 11	Means of verbal discourse variables by age group	78
Figure 12	Means of nonverbal discourse variables by age group	79

LIST OF PHOTOS

Photo 1	An older sibling teaches a toddler how to feed maize stalks to cows	55
Photo 2	Use of task simplification. The older sibling simplifies the task by breaking the maize stalk into bits instead of giving the whole maize stalk to the toddler	55
Photo 3	Guiding the toddlers' body. An older sibling holds a toddler's hands so he can show her the correct way one should hold ones fingers when singing a certain song	56
Photo 4	The older sibling now teaches the toddler how to sing and wave her hands	56
Photo 5	Guiding the toddlers' body. An older sibling holds a toddlers' hand so he can guide her in shaking another toddlers' hand	57
Photo 6	Nonverbal aggressive behaviour. An older sibling kicks a bench that a toddler is holding	58
Photo 7	Nonverbal aggressive behaviour. An older sibling throws a bench at a toddler	58
Photo 8	Nonverbal aggressive behaviour. An older sibling continues to hit a toddlers' palm with a stick even when the toddler shows clear signs of feeling pain	59
Photo 9	Nonverbal possessiveness. An older sibling holds a plastic bottle up and away from a toddler so the toddler is not able to reach it	60
Photo 10	Nonverbal possessiveness. Now the older sibling holds the plastic bottle behind her back as the toddler continues trying to reach it	60
Photo 11	Nonverbal possessiveness. The older sibling has now placed the plastic bottle under her armpit to ensure the toddler can not reach it	61
Photo 12	An older sibling teaching a toddler how to play a ball game	61

Photo 13 Talk with demonstration. An older sibling uses talk
with demonstration to show a toddler how he should
kick a ball 62

Photo 14 Talk with demonstration. An older sibling uses
talk with demonstration while teaching a toddler
how to dance 62

CHAPTER I
INTRODUCTION

1.1 Background of the study

Mothers are the primary caretakers of small children in almost all societies. However, multiple caretaking arrangements exist in non-western societies with other members of the household and the community assisting the mother in child care. Various studies have revealed the existence of multiple-caretaking in diverse societies ranging from agrarian communities such as the Zinacantec Maya of Mexico (Maynard, 1999), the Embu (Whaley, Sigman, Beckwith, Cohen & Espinosa, 2002) and Gusii of Kenya (Levine, 2002), to foraging communities such as the Efe of Democratic Republic of Congo (Tronick, Morelli & Ivey, 1992), Agta of the Philippines (Estioko-Griffen & Griffen, 1981), Aka of the Central African Republic (Hewlett, 1988), Tiwi of Australia (Goodale, 1971) and Adaman Islanders (Radcliffe-Brown, 1964). Multiple caretaking is utilized to such a large extent that children receive less care by their mothers when there are many potential caretakers (Munroe & Munroe, 1971).

The majority of the multiple caretakers tend to be female adult relatives and female children (Levine, 2002; Weisner & Gallimore, 1977) but male children are also to be found taking care of younger children especially during the early childhood years when caretaking responsibilities are shared among both sex peer groups (Weisner & Gallimore, 1977). Older children are therefore engaged in sibling caretaking (Levine et. al, 1994; Maynard, 1999; Munroe & Munroe, 1971; Rabain-Jamin, Maynard & Greenfield, 2003; Rindstedt, 2001; Weisner, 1982, 1989; Weisner & Gallimore, 1977; Wenger, 1989; Whiting & Edwards, 1988; Whittemore & Beverly, 1989; Zukow, 1989). Subsistence based horticultural and or pastoral societies normally make greatest use of children as child caretakers (Konner, 1976).

Sibling caretaking comprises a large portion of children's daily activities. Two to four year olds have been reported to spend more than 70 percent of everyday under the care of child nurses (Best &

Williams, 1997). Thus, younger children participate in socio-cultural activities through their older siblings imitation of their parents caretaking styles. However, they also modify these styles to some degree (Rogoff, 2003). In the interactions between older and younger siblings during sibling caretaking, younger siblings learn various values, knowledge, and skills from their sibling caretakers (Cicirelli, 1994). Therefore, the older siblings may intentionally or unintentionally transmit culture to the younger children. According to the National Academy of Sciences (1994), cultural variables will influence how children present themselves, understand the world, and interpret experiences. Caretaking of small children thus implies transmitting cultural values to the children in everyday context during everyday activities.

1.2 Statement of the problem

It can be assumed that siblings and other family members play a great role in any child's life. It is therefore important to study the social networks in toto when studying children's development. Most of the research conducted in the past on sibling relationships has focused on how younger children learn from older siblings. Very little research has been conducted in the area of sibling teaching and even the few studies that have been carried out so far did not focus on children's teaching over a cross-section of ages. In addition, these other studies did not focus on sibling teaching during children's daily activities. To date, the only study that has described and examined the development of teaching skills over a cross-section of ages during daily activities was that conducted by Maynard (1999). There is therefore a need to carry out more research examining the development of teaching skills during sibling interactions and thus analyse the structure and discrepancies of cultural teaching of toddlers by older siblings.

More research on daily routines and everyday activities in different cultural environments is therefore also required. Harkness and Super (2002) emphasize that the assessment of daily routines and everyday activities has escaped researchers' attention in spite of the fact that daily routines or everyday activities are a rich source of information about individuals and their cultural milieu.

Psychology is a fairly new concept in Kenya and literature on Kenyan psychological and socialization patterns is lacking (Koinange, 2001). During the last decades, the view has been accepted that human development differs across cultural contexts. Thus universal developmental tasks have to be analysed with respect to culture specific solutions (Keller & Greenfield, 2000; Rabain-Jamin et. al, 2003). There is therefore a crucial gap with respect to psychological issues in Kenya that needs to be addressed.

1.3 Purpose of the Study

The purpose of this study was to investigate sibling teaching among the Agikuyu of Kenya. This study shall contribute to the cultural understanding of children's socialization. At the same time it can contribute to the assessment of the variability of the human condition.

CHAPTER II
CONCEPTUAL FRAMEWORK

2.1 Intergenerational cultural transmission

Societies all over the world strive to socialize their children into competent members by imparting to them the accepted cultural norms and values. These processes imply the transmission of culture. Generally, transmission of culture represents the passing on of norms and values of a people on to new members of that cultural environment. The transmission process covers intentional and nonintentional processes since it is the cultural environment that communicates ways of feeling, thinking and behaving to the growing child (Mead, 1953).

Hewlett and Lamb (2002) view culture as transmitted non-genetically from generation to generation through vertical and horizontal transmission of cultural mechanisms. They describe vertical transmission as being most frequent during infancy and early childhood while horizontal transmission occurs during early childhood, between generations and also in late childhood and adolescence within generations.

Vertical transmission is seen as prevalent in slow changing, subsistence-based societies while horizontal transmission occurs in complex and fast changing societies. "Semes" which are specific culturally transmitted units are used to differentiate between the two transmission mechanisms. Semes include schema, knowledge and practices (Hewlett, de Silvertri & Guglielmino, 2002).

In the vertical transmission mechanism, the child learns from his or her parents while the horizontal mechanism is one where the child picks information from unrelated individuals. Infant care giving practices is one of the examples Hewlett & Lamb (2002) provide to better illustrate the two cultural transmission mechanisms. Aka foragers and Ngandu farmers of the Central African Republic reported having learnt their infant care giving practices from their parents and they usually knew these skills by the age of ten (Hewlett & Cavalli Sforza, 1988). On the other hand, Euro-American parents rely on books, paediatricians or close friends for advice on infant care giving practices. Therefore, information on child care among Euro-Americans appears to be transmitted by horizontal transmission while vertical transmission appears to be one of the principle mechanisms by which infant care knowledge is transmitted among the Aka and Ngandu who are subsistence based societies.

While vertical and horizontal transmission mechanisms may be some of the ways in which cultural transmission occurs, other researchers (Greenfield, 2002) argue that genes play a role in transmission of culture. To illustrate this viewpoint, Greenfield (2002) cites the example of genetically related but environmentally unrelated groups such as the Zinacantec Maya of Mexico and other Asian groups such as Chinese-Americans who have been found to share behavioural qualities (Freedman, 1979; Freedman & Freedman, 1969). One of the behavioural qualities they share is long visual attention spans which seems to lay the foundation for later observational learning (Brazelton, Robey & Collier, 1969) especially among the Zinacantec. Zinacantec girls for example had the ability to observe their adult teachers attentively for long periods of time when learning to weave (Greenfield, Brazelton & Childs, 1989).

Greenfield (2002) further argues that cultural environments reinforce genetic states while transmitting culture. Haviland (1978) for example observed that pregnant women among the Zinacantec Maya provided their unborn babies with a restrained style of prenatal movement environment that itself was culturally mandated and which most probably reinforced genetic motor patterns. Zinacantecan cultural practices such as swaddling (Brazelton et. al, 1969; Greenfield, 1972) and nursing at the slightest sign of movement (Brazelton et al., 1969) further reinforced newborn's quiet motor behaviour. There was also evidence of low motor activity in older children who sat observing for long periods of time as they learnt how to weave (Childs & Greenfield, 1980; Greenfield, 1984) and this low level of physical activity continued into adulthood with Zinacantecan women never engaging in sweeping, expansive gestures nor allowing their limbs to stray outward from their bodies (Haviland, 1978).

Greenfield (2002) also proposes that cultures have practices that respect and stimulate sensitive periods for cognitive and neural development. There is for example, a developmental timing and order to which Zinacantec girls are exposed to weaving tools. They start on a toy loom at age three and do not set up a real loom before age six at the earliest. This in effect implies the girls are only allowed to handle the real looms when their capabilities have increased with age. In summary, Greenfield (2002) proposes that culture can be presumed to reinforce biology while at the same time it respects biology.

Other researchers (Keller & Greenfield, 2000) propose that parenting styles will also play a role in intergenerational cultural transmission as parenting styles may lead to diverging developmental pathways. Keller and Eckensberger (1998) and Greenfield and Suzuki (1998) have identified pathways which may be termed individualism and collectivism, independence and interdependence, or autonomy and relatedness (Greenfield, 1994; Kagitcibasi, 1996; Markus & Kitayama, 1991).

Triandis (1995) makes a distinction between individualism and collectivism by describing individualistic societies as those that give priority to personal goals, focus on personal needs and rights, and emphasize on maintaining relationships only if they are personally advantageous. Collectivistic societies on the other hand are described as those giving priority to group goals, which focus on norms and duties, and emphasize maintaining interpersonal relationships. The assumption is that independent societies are found in European-derived and industrial, urban or commercial societies while interdependent ones are to be found in rural environments in Africa, Asia and Latin America.

Parenting styles that foster warmth and closeness can be assumed to lead to interdependence or collectivism while those that encourage a face-to-face exchange between the caregiver and the infant lead to independence or individualism (Greenfield, 2002). In the interdependent or collectivism pathway, the main socialization context is established through body proximity thus promoting warmth and interrelatedness. This developmental pathway continues to socialize skills through observation and participation, finally leading to an interdependently acquired self (Markus & Kitayama, 1991). On the other hand, in the independent or individualistic pathway which emphasizes the universal face-to-face system, the mother orients the child from early on to the material world and tends to use toys when interacting with the child. Socialization for the development of technological intelligence takes place since this pathway encourages the development of the child's inborn reaction to objects. Infants early culturally defined learning is thus part of an intergenerational transmission process of norms and values, based in biological predispositions (Keller 2002).

Keller and Greenfield (2000) further argue that care giving arrangements carry cultural meaning. When an infant is given toys to play with on his or her own, object behaviour is culturally emphasized. The infant learns the cultural value of independence but in contrast, person behaviour is culturally emphasized when an infant is given other people to play with as this infant learns through experience the cultural value of interdependence. Having different caretaking arrangements therefore implies transmitting different cultural values to the child.

Although the various researchers discussed here may have different views as to how cultural transmission occurs, one thing they have in common and that they highlight is the role of the older members of the community as cultural transmitters. This refers especially to those people the child comes into contact with daily such as his or her caretakers who may include parents, siblings or in certain communities, the extended family. Through constant interaction with these individuals in everyday contexts, the child learns what is expected of him or her (Rogoff, 2003; Greenfield, Keller, Fulgni, & Maynard, 2003).

Therefore, there exist various views on how cultural transmission takes place. However, despite the existence of different views on cultural transmission, one thing that remains clear is that transmission of culture is an important aspect of every social order. Most societies insist on individuals adopting existing norms in order to be accepted and some researchers (Tomasello, Kruger & Ratner, 1993) have argued that any child who does not learn the cultural traditions of his or her culture would simply not be considered a normal member of the group. Since cultural transmission is a very crucial element of every culture, it is also important to understand the different ways in which it may occur, namely through cultural learning and cultural teaching.

2.2 Cultural learning and cultural teaching

2.2.1 Cultural learning

Tomasello et al. (1993) discuss a universal pattern of cultural learning which they describe as a uniquely human form of social learning where behaviour and information are transmitted within and across generations in a manner that is not seen in other animal species. They argue that the reason human beings are able to do this is because they have the ability to understand and take the perspective of others that is, human beings attempt to see a situation the way others see it. In addition, they propose that children acquire a particular cultural learning skill at around the same time they are showing evidence of the logically related social-cognitive skill. That is, children acquire behaviours which seem to form a basis for the particular cultural learning skill to take place. The three types of cultural learning processes they describe are imitative, instructed and collaborative learning.

Imitative learning is presumed to appear in the second half year of the infants' life. For this type of learning to take place, the child has to understand what the other person or model perceives and intends. Infants object directed actions and use of communicative symbols at this age is a clear indication that they engage in imitative learning.

Research (Abravanel & Gringold, 1985; Masur & Ritz, 1984; Mccall, Parke & Kavanaugh, 1977; Meltzoff, 1988a; 1988b) has shown that infants in the second half year of life are able to imitatively learn novel object-directed actions after observing adults and the fact that the infants use these behaviours in novel situations is a clear indication that they engage in imitation and are not just mimicking. That is, the infants have understood the adults' goals and are not just reproducing the adults' behaviour.

It is also during the second half year of life that infants start to learn conventional linguistic symbols. Conventional linguistic symbols can only be learned imitatively and their use in appropriate novel situations provides further evidence that infants imitative learning skills begin at around this age.

Infants at this age also display new behaviours that would help explain their tendency to imitate other persons. These new behaviours such as engaging in joint attention with people indicate the infants are able to distinguish between inanimate objects and they view persons as intentional agents. Viewing people as intentional agents means they view people as having a purpose or reason. Infants perception of persons as intentional agents would therefore explain their tendency to imitate them. As stated earlier on, for an infant to be able to imitate, he or she must understand what the other person or model perceives and intends. Once the child can see a situation from the perspective of the model, he or she can then reproduce both means and ends in one imitative act for himself or herself.

Cultural learning therefore occurs once a child can take the perspective of others. This is even clearer in the manner in which children learn conventional linguistic symbols. Tomasello (1992) points out that children in their second year of life learn verbs as adults are either telling them what to do or anticipating their impending actions. This means perspective taking will play a big role as the children have to understand the adults' intentions in a way that allows them to determine the adults focus of attention. In brief, imitative learning can be described as relying on a concept of intentional agent and involving simple perspective-taking. It is therefore a form of cultural transmission where valued elements of a culture are transmitted.

Instructed learning is also a form of cultural transmission, but it also involves teaching. Basically learners internalize the instructions of the instructor and later on use them to self-regulate their own cognitive functions. That is, the learners later on repeat the others instructions when confronted with the same or a similar situation. This reproduction of the others instructions is a clear indication that the learner has paid attention to the instructions and understood them in the original learning context therefore he or she and the instructor have achieved some form of inter-subjectivity in the task situation. Achieving inter-subjectivity means trying to understand the task or situation from the other persons point of view. Specifically, there is an asymmetrical form of inter-subjectivity that is, both the learner and the other person try at the same time to see each others points of view. In instructed learning the learner learns about the other person specifically, about the others understanding of the task and how that compares with his or her own understanding.

Tomasello et al (1993) presume instructed learning appears in children when they are around four years old since research (Goudena, 1987; Kontos, 1983; Ratner & Hill, 1991) provides evidence that children at this age can internalize adult instructions. This is also the age at which children first show evidence of spontaneous efforts to teach or regulate the learning of others.

Behaviours which seem to form a basis for instructed learning also appear during this age range for example, children at this age use words that refer to the thoughts and knowledge of others and they also deceive others with full knowledge of its effect on the others mental states. They also begin to behave in adult like ways by being able to successfully predict what another child will do when given information that the subject child knows is false (Wimmer & Perner, 1983). This is a clear indication that at this age children realise others have mental states that differ from their own. They therefore view others as mental agents, that is, they view others as having individual thoughts and beliefs that guide their behaviour and which may sometimes be compared and contrasted to the child's own thoughts and beliefs. Instructed learning therefore relies on a concept of mental agent.

These new developments in four year olds therefore imply they have the capability to engage in instructed learning because one of the requirements for instructed learning to take place is that the learner has to be able to understand the instructor's mental perspective and then relate that point of view to his or her own. The learner therefore has to understand and compare his or her and the instructors' perspectives since they may have differing perspectives on the same situation.

Tomasello et al. (1993) further argue that the instructions most likely to be internalised by the learner are those that occur at difficult points in the task, that is, the points at which the learner and the instructor are not focused together on an aspect of the task. The learner becomes aware of this difference as he or she tries to understand the instructor and will therefore tend to try and restore inter-subjectivity. This attempt to restore inter-subjectivity is viewed by Tomasello et al (1993) as taking place in the form of a dialogue. The learner internalises and retains the dialogue which he or she uses in future similar tasks and this is a clear indication that instructed learning is a process of cultural transmission like imitative learning.

Collaborative learning on the other hand, is not viewed as a cultural transmission processes but as a process of co-construction or cultural creation. It is a process of co-construction because in collaborative learning peers work together to construct something new that neither had before the interaction began. An advantage of this is that the individual's creativity is enhanced although in a few instances collaborative learning leads to maintenance of cultural traditions as similar collaborative efforts and solutions are always used for similar situations.

Collaborative learning is also presumed to be symmetrical because neither of the two participants is an expert. It occurs in a symmetrical inter-subjective manner because each collaborator tries to take the perspective of and to learn through the other collaborator. Collaborative learning is of great benefit to school age children as they understand and perform better on a task when they work together with a peer and various studies such as on Piagetian conservation tasks (Ames & Murray, 1982; Doise & Mugny, 1979; Glachan & Light, 1982) and studies of school-age children discussing moral issues (Kruger & Tomasello, 1986) provide evidence of the same.

Tomasello et al. (1993) believe it is at six to seven years old that children acquire the socio-cognitive base necessary for collaborative learning. It is at this age that they display a changing conception of a person for example, at this age, they are able to reflect on what others may be thinking. Collaborative learning therefore relies on a concept of reflective agent.

Another feature of collaborative learning is the presence of recursive interaction that is, a collaborator must be able to criticize the other collaborator's criticism of their previous suggestion if they are to engage in a co-construction process. This sort of interaction is necessary so that the perspectives of both parties may be included. Collaborative learning therefore not only relies on a concept of reflective agent but also involves integrated perspective taking.

Research (Kruger & Tomasello, 1986; Mugny & Doise, 1978) shows children begin to use reflective and recursive language spontaneously when they are about six to seven years which is also the same age that they engage in reflective and recursive dialogues and co-construction. These entire skills enable the child understand the reflective agents' mental perspectives and this is the basis for collaborative learning. Therefore, for collaborative learning to take place, a child must understand the collaborators reflective thoughts and beliefs so as to be able to carry on the reflective dialogue necessary for collaboration and also to engage in the recursive mental-state language. Therefore, there has to be recursive intersubjectivity for collaborative learning to take place.

These three types of cultural learning processes that Tomasello et al. (1993) discuss seem to follow a developmental process, that is the ability to engage in perspective taking seems to be a pre-condition for being able to engage in co-ordinated perspective taking which seems also to be a necessary pre-condition for being able to take the others perspective and learn through the other collaborator. This in effect means that for collaborative learning to take place imitative learning should first occur, which should then be followed by instructed learning.

Other researchers (Rogoff, Mistry, Göncü & Mosier, 1993) propose that new members in any society will learn of the community activities through guided participation. Guided participation is described as a process where children's development occurs through the children's active participation in culturally structured activity with the guidance, support, and challenge of companions who vary in skill and status.

Guided participation appears to be widespread in different cultural communities around the world. Rogoff et. al (1993) provide examples of craft apprenticeship in weaving (in Guatemala and Mexico) and in tailoring (in Liberia), learning the skills of cultivation, animal husbandry, hunting and fishing (in Venezuela), and learning to distinguish between right and left hands for eating during the toddler years (in India) as instances where guided participation takes place (Freed & Freed, 1981; Greenfield, 1984; Greenfield & Lave, 1982; Rogoff, 1986; Ruddle & Chesterfield, 1978). The more skilled members segment and structure the process to be learned, provide guidance during joint activity, and help adjust participation according to increasing skill.

Fortes (1938/1970) states that it is with the guidance of caregivers and companions that children participate in and begin to manage the cultural activities that surround them. Rogoff et. al. (1993) further point out that although guided participation is widespread in different communities, it will occur with cultural variations. In communities where observation of adult activities is encouraged or allowed, children may develop largely through their own initiative, through active observation and gradually increasing participation. On the other hand, in communities where age segregation and compartmentalization of roles may restrict children's access to adult activities, it may be necessary for adults to present children with a simpler version of adult activities and work to motivate the children to practice these activities. Therefore, the major cultural difference is the extent to which caregivers adjust their activities to children as opposed to the extent to which children are responsible for adjusting to and making sense of the adult world.

In addition, Rogoff, et al. (1993) propose that different communities will have different patterns of attending to competing events due to their cultural features. Competing events can be handled either by attending to them simultaneously, by rapidly alternating attention between them or even by appearing unaware of them. Their presumption is that in non-Western cultures or communities which tend to emphasize learning though observation, children are more likely to share their attention among competing events. On the other hand, in cultures where children can expect others to take responsibility for organizing their learning, the children can concentrate on the activity at hand and rely on others to let them know if they are to shift attention. Studies they conducted among caregivers and toddlers among the Maya in San Pedro, Guatemala and a middle-class urban group in Salt Lake City, United States, provides evidence of this. The Salt Lake caregivers and toddlers were found to be frequently unaware of competing events while the San Pedro caregivers and toddlers could simultaneously attend to competing events. Similar results were also obtained by Verhoef & Morelli (submitted) in a study among the Efe of Central Africa and Salt Lake caregivers and toddlers.

Cultural learning as described by Tomasello et al. (1993) and guided participation as put forward by Rogoff et al. (1993) are similar in that both view imitation as a fundamental aspect for cultural transmission to occur. Tomasello et al. (1993) believe infants learn through imitation just as Rogoff et al. (1993) state that children will imitate adult activities after observing the adults or after the adults have presented simplified versions of adult activities to them. Both Tomasello et al. (1993) and Rogoff et al. (1993) also deem mature members in the community as playing a central role by being role models or instructors to younger members.

On the other hand, some differences exist between Tomasello's et al. (1993) and Rogoff's et al. (1993) viewpoints. Tomasello et al. (1993) state cultural learning can only take place once a child can take the perspective of others while Rogoff et al. (1993) propose the child has to receive guidance during joint activity after the process to be learned has been segmented and structured by more skilled members. Tomasello et al. (1993) also discuss collaborative learning in their cultural learning theory where they deem peers as working together to construct something new that neither had before the interaction began while on the other hand Rogoff et al. (1993) view one of the participants as being more skilled in the task at hand.

Therefore, in conclusion, cultural learning can be regarded as the process where the younger members of a society learn of the community's ways from the older members of the society. Cultural learning is therefore a very important aspect in the transmission of culture but it is not the only aspect that is necessary for cultural transmission to take place as cultural teaching also has a role to play. Since the capacity to teach is basic to the transmission of human culture (Maynard, 1999), it is also important to look at the role it plays in cultural transmission.

2.2.2 Cultural teaching

Cultural teaching has been depicted as focusing on the examination of the local discourse practices, the social ecology of development, and the material aspects of the environment that make cultural learning possible (Maynard, 1999). Cultural teaching therefore focuses on the rituals, routines, cultural practices, and socializing agents that support cultural learning. It can be thought of as the system of socialization that exists to support learners in acquiring cultural knowledge of various sorts (Maynard & Greenfield (in press).

For children to be able to engage in cultural teaching and therefore act as cultural transmitters, they have to develop certain skills. Cognitive and socio-cognitive skills (Piaget, 1952, 1967; Rogoff, 1990), linguistic competence (Goodluck, 1991), and inter-subjectivity skills (Gopnik & Meltzoff, 1994; Trevarthen & Logotheti, 1989) that children develop during their preschool years increase the children's ability to teach (Maynard, 1999).

Scaffolding is another important skill that children have to develop. Scaffolding has been described as a process where more competent members of a culture provide enough help and support so that the less competent members will not fail at the task, yet not so much that the less competent members will not be challenged (Wood, Bruner & Ross, 1976). Younger siblings will therefore learn through their social interactions with older siblings who provide scaffolding in various activities. Older siblings especially are excellent teachers to their younger siblings because they are related, are often emotionally close, and are close in age (Meisner & Fisher, 1980). Research (Azmitia & Hesser, 1993; Cicirelli, 1972a) even shows that children taught by siblings perform better than those taught by peers.

Various researchers have carried out studies focusing on sibling teaching. Some researchers (Azmitia & Hesser, 1993; Cicirelli, 1972b, 1973; Hancock & Kaiser, 1996; Klein, Feldman & Zarur, 2002; Klein, Zarur & Feldman, 2003; Stewart, 1983) carried out laboratory studies where they asked older siblings to teach the younger children a cognitive or construction task. Other researchers (Cicirelli, 1976) compared mother-child teaching with sibling teaching while other researchers (Volk, 1999) just focused on one family where a Puerto Rican kindergartners' older siblings teaching strategies were compared to those used by the kindergarteners' teacher.

Maynard (1999) on the other hand not only examined sibling teaching per se, but also focused her study on the way cultural teaching develops in children's daily routines. In a study she conducted among the Zinacantec Maya of Nabenchauk on sibling teaching, she observed that cultural teaching took place even in the context of children's play. Older siblings were observed teaching younger siblings how to become competent members of their culture by guiding the younger siblings in cultural activities. Rabain-Jamin et al. (2003) also observed the presence of teaching interaction during play among Wolof siblings of Senegal. Therefore, in the course of their sibling interactions, Wolof and Zinacantec children taught everyday activities such as cooking or taking care of babies through play. The older siblings gave the toddlers tasks to do, drew the toddlers attention to the tasks, or provided models the toddlers could learn from (Rabain-Jamin et al. (2003).

Nevertheless, children are not the only individuals who engage in cultural teaching. Parents have also been perceived of as "trainers" (Harkness & Super, 1995) and various studies (Jahoda, 1982; Middleton, 1970) have labelled childrearing customs "education" and also see parents as playing a role in this training. Studies based on this perspective have focused on the detailed description of processes through which adult culture is transmitted to children, and how educational practices have signalled the demands of adult life. Other researchers (Greenfield & Lave, 1982) studied how girls in a Zinacantecan community of Mexico learnt to weave as they received instructions from their mothers while B. B.

Whiting and Edwards (1988) reported how Ngeca mothers of Kenya believed they should train their children in motor development.

Therefore, parents play a very important role as cultural transmitters to children. The same can also be said of older siblings as they also play an important role in transmission of culture to their younger siblings. This is especially so in many non-western cultures where older siblings are considered as culture brokers who may be as influential or even more influential than parents in socializing young children (Weisner, 1989; Whiting & Edwards, 1988). The relationship between siblings and the interaction between them is therefore of great importance if effective sibling teaching is to take place. Indeed, the uniqueness of the sibling relationship has led researchers to acknowledge that this relationship is one of the most potentially important influences on a child's development (Dunn, 1988, 2000; Newman, 1996). It is therefore important to look at the role of siblings and the interaction between them.

2.3 Sibling interaction

Different societies have different views as to who should be regarded as a sibling. In industrialized societies, siblings are identified by genealogical or biological criteria whereas in non-industrialized societies, siblings may be defined by extension of the term to certain types of blood kin, or by classification on the basis of criteria other than genealogical criteria alone (Cicirelli, 1994). In non-industrialized societies therefore, other individuals such as cousins may be viewed as siblings. However, regardless of which view is held as to who a sibling is, siblings in both industrialized and non-industrialized societies play a significant role in children's lives.

Siblings provide comfort, companionship and support (Cicirelli, 1996; Furman & Buhrmester, 1985a, 1985b; Pepler, Corter & Abramovitch, 1983), help children learn many skills including social-cognitive skills (Brown & Dunn, 1992; Cicirelli, 1996; Deater-Deckard, Dunn & Lussier, 2002; Dunn, Brown & Beardsall, 1991; Dunn, Brown, Slomkowski, Tesla & Youngblade, 1991; Howe, 1991; Howe & Ross, 1990; Klein, et. al, 2002; MacDonald & Parke, 1984; Youngblade & Dunn, 1995), play a part in communicative development (Dunn & Shatz, 1989; Hoff-Ginsberg & Krueger, 1991;

Tomasello, Conti-Ramsden & Ewert, 1990), contribute toward development of leadership and teacher roles (Katz, Kramer & Gottman, 1992; Stoneman & Brody, 1993), are useful in the development of self-identity (Bank & Kahn, 1982; Dunn, 1983) and help enhance self-esteem (Yeh & Lempers, 2004). Siblings therefore have multiple influences on children's cognitive, social and emotional development.

Siblings influence on each other is therefore considerable and older siblings seem to have an even greater influence on younger siblings than younger siblings on older ones (Counts, 1985; Matsumoto, Kudoh & Takeuchi, 1996; Rabain-Jamin et al., 2003), probably because younger siblings greatly admire them (Buhrmester, 1992; Buhrmester & Furman, 1990), viewing them as models, superiors or pacesetters and as sources of strength and pride (Cicirelli, 1994; Gershaw, 1989; Sharma, 1996). Older siblings also have greater capabilities (Gregory, 2002) therefore younger siblings view them as approachable sources of knowledge and advice (Tucker, Barber & Eccles, 1997) and also as teachers and helpers (Abramovitch, Corter, Pepler & Stanhope, 1986; Azmitia & Hesser, 1993; Brody, Stoneman & MacKinnon, 1982; Brody, Stoneman, MacKinnon & Mackinnon, 1985; Dunn & Kendrick, 1982; Furman & Buhrmester, 1985b; Katz et. al, 1992; Stoneman, Brody & MacKinnon, 1986; Vandell & Bailey, 1992; Van Volkom, 2003).

Older siblings capabilities may even make some children have so much faith in them that they will believe them more than their parents (Sharma, 1996) and also appreciate their advice more than that given by friends when mastering tasks (Azmitia & Hesser, 1993; Keller, 2000; Pepler, Abramovitch & Corter, 1981). In addition, their more advanced capabilities result in the expectation that they help younger siblings (Harkness & Super, 2002) and also teach, help, protect and care take younger siblings (Mendelson, Villa, Fitch & Goodman, 1997). Older children due to their more advanced capabilities would therefore be expected to provide more help and research (Azmitia & Hesser, 1993) has also provided evidence of older siblings helping younger ones with play and other tasks where younger siblings assume the role of the learner and follow the example of the older brother or sister. Even in life or death situations, a sibling responsible for her plight would receive more help than a non-responsible acquaintance (Greitemeyer, Rudolf & Weiner, 2003).

Older siblings' tendency to protect and assist their younger ones may originate from a sense of duty especially in the case of African settings where there is a sense of duty in helping among kin (Harkness & Super, 2002). Providing assistance to family members is so highly valued, that some East African communities even provide training for responsibility and helping (Whiting & Edwards, 1988). Training for responsibility therefore takes place with older siblings often being delegated responsibilities for the care of their younger siblings. This type of training for responsibility also seems to also occur in industrialized societies as siblings in these societies are also delegated responsibilities for the care of their younger siblings. However, in industrialized societies, such delegation is carried out informally by parents, primarily to give the parent freedom to pursue other activities but in non-industrialized societies, the objective of sibling caretaking is to allow parents time to fulfil necessary work roles for family survival and maintenance (Cicirelli, 1994).

In the non-industrial communities that employ sibling caretaking, young children spend the best part of the day under older siblings care (Nuckolls, 1993; Rindstedt, 2001; Zukow-Goldring, 1995) with even children as young as five or seven years old taking on the role of sibling caretakers (Levine et. al, 1994; Munroe, Munroe, Michelson, Koel, Bolton & Bolton, 1983; Munroe, Munroe & Shimmin, 1984; Rogoff, Sellers, Pirotta, Fox & White, 1975; Whiting & Edwards, 1988). Research (Ivey, 1992) further reveals that in some communities, infants and toddlers do actually spend a greater percent of their time with siblings than with their fathers. Sibling caretakers therefore play a huge role in young children's lives.

During caretaking sessions, older siblings are in charge and the seniority principle that governs social relations in non-industrial groups officially grants older children authority over their younger siblings (Mendelson et. al, 1997; Rabain-Jamin et al., 2003). Birth order will therefore play a role in sibling relationships (Santrock,

2001) with unequal status in power being conferred by birth order to siblings (Lollis, Van Engen, Burns, Nowack & Ross, 1999). Parents often entrust the first born with power and responsibility (Romeo, 1994) and in non-industrialized societies, cultural norms may establish certain roles for older siblings for example, an older brother may have the greatest seniority and younger siblings are taught to respect older siblings and to obey them as they would a parent (Cicirelli, 1994). Older siblings therefore have higher status.

Younger children look up to older siblings due to their higher status but older siblings sometimes take advantage of the power they have over the younger ones by manipulating the younger ones and sometimes exerting excessive control (Conger, Conger & Scaramella, 1997). Besides manipulation, sibling relations can be marked by conflict (Buhrmester & Furman, 1990; Howe, Rinaldi, Jennings & Petrakos, 2002; Ross et. al., 1996; Vandell & Bailey, 1992; Volling, 2003) with sibling disputes being the most common type of conflict that families face (Straus, Gelles & Steinmetz, 1980).

Sibling conflict is estimated to occur more than six times per hour in families with young children (Dunn & Munn, 1985; Ross, Filyer, Lollis, Perlman & Martin, 1994; Vandell & Bailey, 1992) and when they fight or quarrel, young siblings tend to engage in conflicts that are more contentious and aggressive (McGillicuddy-De Lisi, 1993; Perlman & Ross, 1997; Phinney, 1986). The few studies that have focused on the content of sibling conflict have found that most fights or arguments between siblings revolve around issues on sharing possessions and aggression (Dunn, 1996; Dunn & Kendrick, 1982; Dunn & Munn, 1987; Lollis et. al., 1999; McGuire, Manke, Eftekhari & Dunn, 2000; Prochaska & Prochaska, 1985; Steinmetz, 1977). In addition, when interviewed, siblings themselves have also named sharing personal possessions and physical aggression within their top five conflict areas that is, they reported having disagreements regarding sharing personal possessions and due to physical aggression (McGuire et. al., 2000).

Sibling fights therefore centre on struggles over objects and possessions while some of the verbal aggressive behaviours common among siblings include mocking, teasing, belittling and name-calling (Dunn, 2000; Klein et. al, 2002; Watson-Gegeo &

Gegeo, 1989). Physical aggressive behaviours are just as common (Howe et. al, 2002; McGuire et. al., 2000; Minnett, Vandell & Santrock, 1983; Watson-Gegeo & Gegeo, 1989) with physical aggression being used even on siblings as young as 18 months (Dunn & Munn, 1986). However, use of negative behaviour on siblings reduces as children become older (McGuire et. al., 2000). Negative verbal and physical behaviour is therefore quite common among siblings and siblings seem to direct negative behaviour to each other as they interact.

Sibling interactions therefore seem to be characterised by various activities. Indeed, all these sibling interactions are usually embedded in contexts of play. It is therefore important to look at the different cultural perspectives on play since play is a rich context in which to study sibling interaction (Howe et. al, 2002) and sibling play sessions are sometimes characterised by teaching interactions (Maynard, 1999; Rabain-Jamin, et al., 2003).

2.4 Play in a cultural perspective

Play is one of the most important sources of learning for young children. Learning during play occurs as young children observe and interact with other children who can be viewed as highly skilled members of the culture (Vygotsky, 1967, 1978, 1990). Vygotsky (1978) also adds that play enables children to improve their zone of proximal development. Zone of proximal development was a concept Vygotsky used to explain the differences between the child's independent performance or actual developmental level, and his or her potential development when supported by a more skilled partner. Playing with a more sophisticated partner such as an adult or an older child will therefore enhance a child's skills and encourage more complex play.

It is clear therefore that play is vital for young children's development and older siblings who are children's primary play partners in many communities have a significant role as they are responsible for guiding children's play (Farver, 1993; Farver & Wimbarti, 1995). Research (Farver & Wimbarti, 1995) has even provided evidence that older siblings help children in play by scaffolding the play and encouraging it. However, whether children can play and the amount of time they can play seems to be largely determined by the cultural values of childhood. For example, societies may have definitive views whether children should be protected from adult work or be part of it, and whether or not they should have "a protected social space to play" (Garbarino, 1989).

In urban middle-class communities where parents work outside the home and do not involve children in their economic life, children have few responsibilities other than play and school throughout much of their childhood (Rogoff et al., 1993; Vandermass-Peler, 2002). Parents in these communities view play as an appropriate socialization context and are often the children's play partners (Dunn & Dale, 1984; Farver & Howes, 1993; Farver, Kim & Lee, 1995; Haight & Miller, 1993; Roopnarine, Hooper, Ahmeduzzaman & Pollack, 1993). Parents in these communities also consider play as having developmental and educational significance (Farver & Howes, 1993; Haight & Miller, 1993; Parmar, Harkness & Super, 2004), and may use it as an instructional medium to teach children skills (Göncü, Mistry & Mosier, 2000).

On the other hand, in non-western or low-income communities, children may not have opportunities to play (Gaskins, 1990). In agrarian societies for example, emphasis may be placed on the acquisition of skills that contribute to the economic gain of the family and children perform daily chores and other family responsibilities such as child care (Rogoff et. al., 1993; Vandermass-Peler, 2002). However, even in these societies where children have to work, they have been reported to play as they work or fulfil responsibilities such as sibling caretaking (Rindstedt, 2001; Schwartzman, 1986). Children have also been reported to emulate adult work in their play and this may be an important way for the children to enter into more contributory roles within a few years (Morelli, Rogoff & Angelillo, submitted). Parents in these communities do not view play as important for development (Farver & Howes, 1993; Farver & Wimbarti, 1995; Harkness & Super, 1986; Parmar, et. al., 2004) and children's play partners in these communities may not be adults (Gaskins, 1999; Farver & Howes, 1993). Since children's learning in these communities occurs in the course of their participation in the community activities with adults, adult-child play may be rendered unnecessary with adults even delegating play roles to other children (Rogoff et al., 1993).

Different cultural perspectives on play therefore exist. Göncü, et. al., (2000) argue that these cultural differences are consistent with Kagitcibasi's (1996) description of urban middle-class and subsistence based communities where the former are viewed as encouraging development of independence while the latter are presumed to encourage interdependence. Parents in independent societies will tend to place a lot of value on children's play while parents in interdependent societies may view play as children's business and not have a very high opinion of it. However, different views on the role of play are not the only differing views present between cultures. Many other differences exist. Due to this reason, it is also important to take a look at the Agikuyu people and their way of life in order to have a better understanding of the sibling interactions that may take place among Agikuyu children.

2.5 The Agikuyu people

The Agikuyu people believe they descended from a man called Gikuyu and his wife Mumbi. Gikuyu and Mumbi had nine daughters whose descendants came to be known as the Agikuyu people. The Agikuyu clans (*meherega*) system is based on these daughters with the nine *meherega* being named after Gikuyu and Mumbis' nine daughters. The names of the *meherega* are *Acheera, Agachiko, Airimo, Amboi, Angare, Anjiro, Angoi, Ethaga* and *Aitherando*.

The descendants of these nine daughters belonged to the respective clan of the daughter. Therefore the Gikuyu people believe people belonging to the same clan were related in the past. However, the closest uniting unit among the Agikuyu is the family group (*mbari* or *nyomba*). The *mbari* or *nyomba* consists of a man, his wife, their children and also the grand- and great-grandchildren. Members of one *mbari* or *nyomba* usually live in one homestead especially in the rural areas. The homesteads usually comprise of several houses depending on the number of people of the *mbari* or *nyomba*.

Being an Agrarian community, the Agikuyu people on a normal day will be found working on their farms or engaged in other agricultural activities. However, there are others who are engaged in gainful employment as teachers, civil servants or workers in the private sector. When there is work to be done on the farms, the men and women share the work of cultivating and harvesting crops but there is a clear-cut division of labour regarding certain tasks. Men are the ones normally engaged in repair and maintenance of the houses and livestock sheds while women usually perform the household chores which include cooking, bringing water from the rivers, washing utensils and fetching firewood from the forests. Women are also responsible for caretaking of young children but the Agikuyu society is also one that employs sibling caretaking with girls engaging in sibling caretaking more than boys.

2.5.1 Children's socialization among the Agikuyu

Socialization of young children among the Agikuyu prior to colonial influences was primarily the responsibility of the extended family. Nowadays however, western influences have led to the abandonment of many significant indigenous cultural traditions and the emergence of new practices. One of the most conspicuous changes is the re-organisation of the family structure. Extended family units that were the norm in the past have reduced in number while polygamous families rarely exist. Most families are found as nuclear monogamous units and this has undoubtedly affected socialization patterns with members of the immediate family playing a bigger role in a child's socialization while the extended family influence has dwindled. This however does not imply that there is almost no extended family influence since a sizeable number of extended families can still be found in the rural areas.

In the past, extended family members assisted the child's parents in instructing the children for example, they informed the young children of the family history and community traditions through stories they narrated to them. However, the children's mothers were the primary socialization agents and they could be found informing the very young children of the cultural traditions through songs and lullabies. These songs and lullabies served not only as teaching aids but also as means of soothing and entertaining the children. The children were therefore never informed that they were being educated and ended up internalising their cultural traditions without strain. When the children could talk, they were taught the correct manner of speech and all the important names in the family's past and present while questions were asked from time to time to test how much had been learnt.

When the children started walking, they were also taught how to sit and walk properly. This was also the period when they were taught how to use their hands and both parents took on almost equal responsibility in teaching this task. When the children grew older, the education pattern took on a different approach with fathers taking charge of the boys' education while mothers completely took charge of the girls' education and part of the boys' education.

The young boys accompanied their fathers and other male members of the extended family to the farm where their fathers normally made them digging sticks to play with while they did the actual work. Soon the young boys developed an interest in their fathers' activities and through observation, also learnt how to cultivate. The boys also learnt the names of various plants and roots and their uses and also how to distinguish between edible and poisonous wild fruits and plants. They were also shown how to identify trees that could provide good firewood and also how to identify birds that were harmful to crops and those that could be eaten. Their fathers also pointed out to them the boundaries of the family, clan and tribal lands and also taught them how to develop good observation skills.

Good observation skills and the ability to pay attention to detail were very important for example, individuals were expected to be able to determine the number of animals in a herd without the need of having to count as counting was believed to bring bad luck to the people or animals counted. Individuals therefore had to learn how to differentiate the animals in a herd either by their colour, size, or horns. An example of how good observation skills were fostered is two or three herds from different homesteads were mixed and the young boy receiving training in livestock herding was asked to separate them by picking out all those animals that belonged to his herd. This exercise helped the young boy develop his observation skills, as it was an opportunity for him to practice his abilities when identifying the animals belonging to his herd. Sometimes some of the animals in the herd were hidden and the boy was later on asked to inspect the herd and report back to the person in charge of his training. The boy was then asked to recall the last time he saw any animal he reported as missing. In this way the boys' observation and memory skills were strengthened.

Young girls received training from their mothers and older female members of the extended family on how to perform domestic duties in addition to their training in agricultural matters which was similar to that given to boys by their fathers. Both boys and girls also received training in health related matters for example they were instructed not to touch dead animals in order to avoid infections. Through the use of folklores and legends, mothers also instructed both boys and girls on the laws and customs especially those governing the moral codes and general rules of etiquette in the community. Children for example were taught to give respect and obedience where it was due. Children were to always talk to their parents in a polite tone and also address all adults politely. It was considered impolite to address an adult by his or her name. Children referred to adults as "father of so-and so", "mother of so-and-so", "uncle of so-and-so" or "aunt of so-and-so" when talking to them.

Older siblings were also sometimes left in charge of the younger children when parents went to cultivate fields. They therefore also played a role in the young children's socialization for example, Kenyatta (1965) describes how he underwent training on herding of cattle, sheep and goats and afterwards taught this to his younger brothers. Children therefore received training from parents and older family members and they in turn taught their younger siblings what they had learnt.

Nowadays, a child's mother is his or her primary caretaker when he or she is very young therefore she is still also the young child's primary socialization agent although older siblings are also to be found assisting in childcare. This is especially so during the school holidays and over weekends when parents leave the older children in charge of the younger ones. Sometimes the older children who can already handle farming tools accompany parents to the farms and by watching their parents and also by receiving guidance and instruction from the parents, also learn how to plant and harvest crops.

Socialization of young children among the Agikuyu has therefore undergone various changes due to modernization but some activities such as sibling caretaking and parental guidance on agricultural matters seem to have been carried on to the present.

2.6 Assumptions of the study

The aim of this study was to identify sibling teaching that may occur as siblings interacted in the course of their daily activities. Although some research had been carried out in the area of sibling teaching, these previous studies apart from that of Maynard (1999) did not focus on sibling teaching that may occur during daily activities. The findings of this study will therefore contribute to existing knowledge as the study provides more literature on sibling teaching during siblings daily routine interactions.

In addition, previous studies on sibling teaching apart from that of Maynard (1999) and Rabain-Jamin et. al, (2003) were not carried out in societies which can be regarded as non-industrial. Nevertheless, even the Rabain-Jamin et. al (2003) study was carried out in a West African country while the present study was done in an East African country, specifically in Kenya among the Agikuyu people who like many non-industrial communities, employ sibling caretaking.

As discussed earlier, sibling caretaking is regarded as one of the ways in which training for responsibility and helping is carried out in many East African communities. Helping is highly valued and there is a sense of duty in helping among kin with older children due to their more advanced capabilities being socialized to help younger siblings. The first assumption of this study is therefore derived from this literature and it states:

Assumption 1

It is assumed that the older siblings would try to help or assist the toddlers with older children providing more assistance to the toddlers than younger children. This might be the case especially in situations where the toddlers due to limited capabilities are unable to perform certain tasks.

The assumption above therefore implies that older siblings would help younger siblings. This study went a step further as it also attempted to identify help that may occur in sibling teaching during daily activities since no study so far has set out to establish if children do actually help younger siblings during interactions in daily activities. Previous studies have only focused on older siblings helping younger siblings in play but they did not try to identify the help that may occur in sibling teaching during daily activities.

The literature reviewed further reveals that younger children among the Agikuyu are socialized to respect their elders. This implies that older siblings expect younger siblings to obey them therefore if older siblings feel younger siblings are not obeying them, they might try to manipulate the younger siblings since previous studies also show they have greater influence on their younger siblings than the younger siblings have influence over them. Older siblings may therefore use more manipulation than younger siblings. The second assumption is derived from this viewpoint and it states:

Assumption 2

It is assumed that the older siblings would seek to manipulate or exert control over the toddlers with older children trying to manipulate the toddlers more than the younger children especially in situations where the toddlers do not obey them. This is because the seniority principle governing social relations in non-industrial groups officially grants older children authority over their younger siblings therefore the older siblings would expect the toddlers to obey them.

The above assumption therefore suggests older siblings manipulate younger siblings. However, although there are studies proving older siblings have influence over younger siblings none of these studies unlike the present study tried to identify the different ways in which older siblings would try to manipulate younger siblings as siblings interacted during their daily activities. The findings of this study may therefore help fill this gap.

Older siblings' manipulation of younger siblings may end up as being excessive control which may lead to siblings directing negative behaviour to each other as literature has provided evidence that siblings display negative behaviour to each other with younger children displaying more negative behaviour. The third assumption is therefore derived from this literature and it states:

Assumption 3

It is assumed that the older siblings would direct negative behaviour towards the toddlers with younger children displaying more negative behaviour than older children. This would be the case especially in situations where the older siblings feel the toddlers are not obeying them.

This assumption implies that older siblings target negative behaviour at younger siblings. However, previous studies unlike the present study did not try to determine if older siblings display negative behaviour to younger siblings during sibling teaching as the siblings interact in their daily activities. The findings of this study may therefore provide more literature in this area.

In summary, it can be stated that this study will contribute to existing knowledge because its findings when compared to previous findings may provide an idea of some of the discrepancies that are present in cultural teaching of younger siblings by older siblings.

CHAPTER III
METHODOLOGY

3.1 Study site

Gatundu North division of Thika district in the Central Province of Kenya was the study site. Gatundu North division was selected for the study because it provided a fairly homogeneous rural community. Most of the families in the area live as extended families although there are also quite a number of nuclear families.

Families usually live in homesteads which are located on their farms with the houses in the homesteads ranging from semi-permanent mud walled houses to stone walled permanent houses. A number of iron sheet houses are also to be found in the area. Iron sheets are also the most popular roofing materials although a few houses have traditional grass thatched roofs.

A handful of the stone walled houses have an electricity supply but firewood, charcoal and kerosene remain the major sources of energy in all homesteads. Sources of water include rivers and underground water in the form of boreholes therefore there is an abundant supply of water. This abundant water supply may be attributed to the geographical location of the district.

3.1.1 Geographical location, topography and climate

Thika district is situated approximately 40 kilometres north of Kenya's capital Nairobi. It lies between latitudes 3° 53 and 1° 45 south of the Equator and longitudes 36° 35 and 37° 25 east. It has a diverse topography ranging from 1060 m to 3550 m above sea level with an average altitude of about 1524 metres above sea level.

The topographic features have affected climatic conditions leading to temperatures varying during the year with a mean minimum of 8°C and a mean maximum of 30°C. The mean temperature of the district is 20°C with the coldest months being June, July and August and the hottest being February, March and April. There is also a bi-modal rain pattern with long rains occurring in the months of March to May and short-rains in the months of October to December.

Rainfall ranges from 965 mm to 2130 mm and these rainfall patterns have had an influence on some of the economic activities in the area.

3.1.2 Economic activities

Economic activities in the area vary with the greatest number of individuals being engaged in agricultural activities while others are engaged in gainful employment in the adjoining Thika town. The economic development of the area seems to have been greatly influenced by topographic features for example, the suitable climate has encouraged many people to engage in coffee farming and growing of subsistence crops such as maize, beans and potatoes. A small minority also engage in livestock keeping which mostly consists of cattle rearing for the production of milk. All these agricultural activities are in line with the economic activities that the Agikuyu people have always been associated with.

Figure 1 Location of Thika in Kenya

3.1.3 District inhabitants and population

The Agikuyu people who are the largest ethnic group in Kenya are the greatest number of inhabitants of the district. The 1999 Population and Housing Census results released in 2000 revealed that Kenya had a population of 28.7 million with the Agikuyu people numbering over 5.3 million (The Daily Nation, February 18 2000). The census results also showed that Thika district had a population of 645,713 people with an estimated annual growth rate of 2.8 per cent (Kenya Ministry of Finance and Planning, 2002).

3.2 Time of study

The data collection phase was undertaken from November 2002 to February 2003. This period was proposed because Kenyan children have the longest school holiday from November to January each year. Since one of the aims of this study was to examine cultural teaching by older siblings, it was important to collect the data when the older siblings were at home and possibly engaged in caretaking of the toddlers. The period November 2002 to February 2003 was therefore the most ideal for data collection.

3.3 Delimitations of the study

Cultural teaching is a very vast concept but due to special interests and practical constraints such as limited time, the study was delimited to teaching of toddlers by older siblings as the siblings interacted with each other. The sample size was also relatively small and confined only to Gatundu North division of Thika district. Unlike previous studies that focused only on sibling teaching, this study also focused on sibling teaching during daily activities.

3.4 Sample frame

The sample frame included 67 older siblings and 34 toddlers. The older siblings were aged between three and a half and eleven and a half years and included 38 girls and 29 boys. The toddlers were all around two years old with their ages ranging from 20 to 33 months. There was an equal number of toddlers according to gender that is, there were 17 boys and 17 girls.

Two year olds were chosen for this study because two years is the age at which children begin to enjoy playing near other children and also join in others play activities (Malley, 1991). It was expected that the two year olds in the selected sample would be engaged in play with older siblings.

At two years, children have a vocabulary of several hundred words therefore can communicate with other children through the use of two to three word sentences (Malley, 1991). Having a sample consisting of toddlers who can communicate is also important when qualitative data analysis of verbal discourse variables is to be undertaken. Two year olds also begin to engage in simple dramatic make-believe play involving the home and will engage in imitation especially of their parents and guardians. They also have a great interest in learning how to use common items therefore they provide an ideal sample for studying how cultural teaching takes place.

The number of older brothers or sisters each toddler had ranged from none to seven with a mean of 1.6 brothers, sisters or both. Although some toddlers did not have brothers or sisters, they were living in the same homestead with other relatives such as cousins who were considered as siblings. Most of the siblings that is 94.1% lived in the same homestead as the toddler. Only 5.8% lived in other homesteads that is, 2.9% lived with their father in another homestead and the other 2.9% were married in other homesteads. The number of other relatives apart from brothers and sisters living in the same homestead as the toddlers ranged from 2 to 20 with a mean of 6.7 relatives.

Most of the toddlers' parents were middle aged and mothers ages ranged from 18 to 46 with a mean of 27 years 3 months while the ages of the fathers which were known ranged from 20 to 50 years with a mean of 32 years 11 months.

All the toddlers' parents had low income generating occupations with the majority of the mothers being peasant farmers while most of the fathers had small scale jobs such as carpenters, mechanics and drivers. Some of the toddlers' mothers also had small scale jobs such as selling fruits at the local market while some fathers made a living as peasant farmers. Unfortunately, some of the fathers' occupations were not known as they had separated from the toddlers mothers and did not live nearby. A detailed description of the toddlers parents' occupations is given in Table 1. As can also be seen in Table 1, most of the toddlers' parents lived together and the toddlers' fathers who were separated from the toddlers' mothers represented only a small proportion of the sample.

Majority of the toddlers' parents only had a basic education as they had only attended primary school while a small proportion had attended high school but there were also some parents who had not been to school. A detailed description of the parents' educational levels can be seen in Table 1.

3.5 Participants

All the participants in the study belonged to the Agikuyu tribe. The Agikuyu community was chosen because like many communities in Kenya, it is a community that employs sibling caretaking with older siblings often young children themselves tending to their younger siblings from infancy.

The participants were recruited on a volunteer basis after a research clearance permit had been obtained from the Ministry of Education, Science and Technology. The researcher and a research assistant approached the selected participants after the research assistant helped identify suitable families having both two-year-old toddlers and older siblings aged between three and a half and eleven and a half years old.

Thirty four homesteads participated in the study. Some homesteads had more than one toddler aged between 20 and 33 months. Where this was the case, only one toddler was taken as the focal child since it was not practical to videotape the same siblings more than once. There were more boy than girl toddlers in the homesteads therefore where there were both a boy and a girl toddler within the required age range, the girl toddler was taken as the focal child. This was done to ensure the final sample did not have too many boy toddlers and not enough girl toddlers. This explains why there was an equal number of boy and girl toddlers in the sample.

Table 1

Socio-demographic Data of Toddlers' Parents

	%
Mothers' occupations	
Peasant farmers	88.2
Small scale jobs	11.8
Fathers' occupations	
Small scale jobs	47.1
Peasant farmers	38.2
Not known	14.7
Marital status	
Married	67.6
Single parent	23.5
Separated or divorced	8.8
Mothers' level of education	
Primary school	76.4
Secondary school	20.6
Not attended school	2.9
Fathers' level of education	
Primary school	50
Secondary school	29.4
University	2.9
Not attended school	2.9
Not known	14.7

Before their consent was sought regarding participation in the study, families in the participating homesteads were briefed on the aims of the study and what the data collection procedure entailed. The aim of the study was given as a study on young children's development but elaborate descriptions of the aims of the study were not provided as this may have interfered with the data collection process if the family members engaged in activities they assumed may have pleased the researcher.

3.6 Instruments of the study

Two research instruments were used in this study. These were a video recorder and an interview schedule.

3.6.1 Video recording

Video recording was done as older siblings interacted with the two year olds. However, before the actual fieldwork began, the researcher and research assistant prepared a schedule for two visits to each home which were not communicated to the families in order to get the most natural situations. The actual data collection was carried out during the second visit while the purpose of the first visit was to familiarise the families with the researchers in order to minimise any disturbances that may have been caused by their presence when the actual videotaping began later on.

During the first visit, the families were briefed about the manner in which the data collection procedure would be carried out and some video recording was done on this day but this data was not included in the data analysed at the end of the study. The families were informed that the main interest of the study was to find out what siblings did during the day when they were together.

The videotaping session was carried out during the second visit for one hour while the siblings interacted. However, videotaping began ten minutes after the researcher and research assistant arrived in the homesteads in order to reduce the intrusive effect of the researchers. Other family members who were in the homesteads but whose ages were not within the required age range were requested to go on with their daily activities as the videotaping took place.

Some family members went on with their usual routines while others sat at a distance and watched the interactions.

During the video recording, the researcher sat silently in one corner of the compound and did the videotaping. The aim of doing this was to minimise intrusive effects but the disadvantage was that the children forgot a videotaping session was taking place, wandered off the scene and ended up interacting with adults, older children and even neighbours children.

The children engaged in a variety of activities during the videotaping sessions. At times they just ran or sat around and at other times they played games such as ball games, rope skipping, hide and seek or played with stones, bottle tops, old car tyres, soil and mud. Some children also integrated song and dance into their play activities while others engaged in pretend play. There were also feeding sessions where older children fed the toddlers or the children ate together from one plate and in some instances the children fed farm animals such as cows and hens.

Although the majority of families having children in the required age range agreed to take part in the study, some parents and grandparents refused to have their children and grandchildren videotaped. Basically, a lack of understanding of why there is a need to carry out research was the main reason for the refusal. Most people in the area were either illiterate or only had a basic education therefore they did not understand that videotaping had to be the main data collection procedure. Some parents and grandparents feared to have the children videotaped because they had a fear of modern technology. They feared that once the video recording had been done, the tapes could be used for witchcraft or black magic purposes in order to cast spells on the children videotaped. There was also the fear that the videotapes could later on be shown to childless couples who would select the children they liked and later on these children would be kidnapped and sold to the childless couples. Due to the above reasons, 15 two year olds who could have been part of this study were not included.

3.6.2 Interview schedule

The interview schedule was administered to the toddlers' mothers and an audio tape recorder was used to record the participants' responses to the questions in the interview schedule. The interview schedule was used to obtain background information about the families included in the study and also information on the social context of care giving for the toddlers.

The interviews were conducted after the videotaping sessions had been carried out to ensure the questions included in the interview schedule did not lead the respondents to encourage the children to display behaviour they thought would please the researcher during the videotaping sessions.

3.7 Teaching episodes

The teaching episodes in the video tapes were extracted from the longer tapes before transcription was carried out. It was important to extract the teaching episodes from the longer tapes because not all the contents of the videotapes were considered to be teaching episodes for example, the children sometimes started to interact with adults or neighbours children in the middle of sibling interactions. From the 34 hours of tape, 14 hours, 43 minutes and 32 seconds of teaching episodes were extracted.

Teaching was defined as any activity the older siblings drew the toddlers' attention to that could have had the possible effect of transmitting cultural knowledge. Therefore both verbal and nonverbal actions were considered as teaching activities. The teaching sessions were considered to have begun when the older siblings verbally or nonverbally tried to get the toddlers attention while the ends of the teaching sessions occurred when either the toddler or the older sibling who was interacting with the toddler left the scene without returning. Teaching episodes were also considered to have come to an end when either of the children changed tasks and began a new episode with a different activity.

The children's interactions were analyzed by qualitative data analysis. Qualitative data analysis was used in order to assess the children's cognitive and socio-cognitive levels as they interacted with each other. The children's discourse was therefore measured by verbal and nonverbal variables. The discourse measures were developed after reading through the transcripts and watching the videotapes to ascertain which verbal and nonverbal variables the children used in their interactions. Some of these variables had also been used by Maynard (1999) in her study.

Quantitative analyses expressed the children's development of verbal and nonverbal teaching abilities while the qualitative examples illustrated the quantitative findings showing how each of the discourse variables was used by children in the different age groups.

3.7.1 Variables used in quantitative analysis

The verbal discourse variables included the words the older siblings said to the toddlers whereas the nonverbal discourse variables were the older siblings actions as they interacted with the toddlers. However, some discourse variables included words and actions and these were put in a third category which was named the verbal, nonverbal or both category. All the discourse variables therefore fell under one of the three categories. In addition, incomplete sentences the older siblings uttered were not coded if no sense could be made out of them.

3.7.1.1 Verbal discourse variables

The verbal discourse variables included commands, praise, feedback, explanations and descriptions.

Commands. Commands are the orders older siblings issued to the toddlers. Examples of commands included statements such as "Come here" and "let go", or "Let me see" as the older sibling requested to see some banana stems that the toddler was holding.

Praise. Praise included all words or phrases the older siblings said which showed approval or admiration of the toddlers. Praise also included instances where older siblings talked of the toddlers' abilities whether directly or indirectly. There was therefore direct praise and indirect praise. An example of direct praise would be when an older sibling said the words "Good girl" or "Good boy" directly to the toddler while an example of indirect praise would be when an older sibling said the words "Lucy (toddler) is not like you.

You (other siblings) are bad!". This statement implied the toddler was good. Another example would be when one older sibling said to another sibling "See Stevo (toddler) is not scared of hens" when the toddler was within earshot.

Feedback. Feedback included instances when the older siblings made positive or negative comments that guided the toddlers' behaviour. It also included instances when older siblings responded to the toddlers' questions. There was therefore positive feedback, negative feedback and feedback to a question. A statement such as "Yes Marcos, like that!" is an example of positive feedback while the words "Not like that!" are an example of negative feedback.

Explanations and descriptions. Explanations and descriptions were all statements uttered by the older siblings to enable the toddlers understand the activities the children were engaged in or words uttered by the older siblings in order to tell the toddlers what something was like or what was going to happen. Some of these statements contained a reason for example when an older sibling took an object from the toddler and said "Bring so that we put it back the way it was". Other statements were of states or outcomes, of anticipated activities or of what was happening. An example of a statement about a state or outcome would be when an older sibling filled a bottle with soil then said "It (bottle) is now full". The words "I will pick you" said by an older sibling when she put her hands around a toddlers' waist would be an example of a statement about an anticipated activity while the words "The shawl is becoming dirty" would be an example of a statement of what was happening.

3.7.1.2 Nonverbal discourse variables

The nonverbal discourse variables included task simplification and guiding the toddlers' body.

Task simplification. Included instances when the older siblings broke tasks into simpler parts so that the tasks were easier for the toddlers for example when an older sibling plucked leaves off a branch and gave the leaves to the toddler rather than handing the whole branch to the toddler.

Guiding the toddlers' body. Instances when the older siblings touched the toddlers' bodies to guide them in performing specific activities for example when an older sibling held a toddler's hands, pushed the toddler's fingers towards her palm and also pushed the toddler's thumb upwards so that the toddler displayed the correct hand gestures in a song and dance game.

Photo 1 :   An older sibling teaches a toddler how to feed maize stalks to cows.

Photo 2 :   Use of task simplification. The older sibling simplifies the task by breaking the maize stalk into bits instead of giving the whole maize stalk to the toddler.

Photo 3: Guiding the toddlers' body. An older sibling holds a toddler's hands so he can show her the correct way one should hold ones fingers when singing a certain song.

Photo 4: The older sibling now teaches the toddler how to sing and wave her hands

Photo 5 : Guiding the toddlers' body. An older sibling holds a toddlers' hand so he can guide her in shaking another toddlers' hand

3.7.1.3 Verbal, nonverbal discourse variables or both

This category contained variables that were verbal, nonverbal or both and these were aggressive behaviour and possessiveness. However, the verbal and nonverbal categories were separated from each other.

Aggressive behaviours. Verbal aggressive behaviours included insulting the toddlers for example when an older sibling said to a toddler "Silly". Also included in verbal aggressive behaviour was using a loud voice to express anger at the toddler that is, screaming at or yelling at the toddler. Saying "Aaaah!" loudly at the toddler is an example of this kind of verbal aggressive behaviour as this sound is usually used among the Agikuyu to express anger. Also included in verbal aggressive behaviours were instances when older siblings used teasing comments to intentionally upset the toddlers for example telling the toddler in a mocking voice "I have grabbed it (an object) from you!". Nonverbal aggressive behaviours included hitting, scratching or any actions carried out by the older siblings that inflicted physical pain on the toddlers for example caning a toddler even when she showed clear signs that she was feeling pain.

Photo 6 : Nonverbal aggressive behaviour. An older sibling kicks a bench that a toddler is holding

Photo 7 : Nonverbal aggressive behaviour. An older sibling throws a bench at a toddler

Photo 8: Nonverbal aggressive behaviour. An older sibling continues to hit a toddlers' palm with a stick even when the toddler shows clear signs of feeling pain.

Possessiveness. Verbal possessiveness included instances where the older siblings refused to share (an) object(s) with the toddlers by telling the toddlers that they would not share for example, while referring to a lid that was lying on the ground between him and a toddler, the older sibling said to the toddler "It (lid) is mine!". Nonverbal possessiveness included all actions carried out by the older siblings which showed possessiveness for example, when an older sibling did not let a toddler hold a bottle. She held it high above her head and then behind her back so that the toddler could not reach it.

Talk with demonstration. Talk with demonstration included instances when the older siblings carried out activities while at the same time describing to the toddlers what was happening or should happen. This included when older siblings described what they were doing for example when an older sibling put her fingers in her mouth like she was putting a doughnut in her mouth, moved her mouth in a chewing motion and said to the toddler "I eat like that". Also included were instances when older siblings described what the toddlers should do for example during a play session with a ball when an older sibling said to a toddler "Hit it (ball) like that!" and also moved her leg backwards and forwards to illustrate to the toddler how he should hit the ball.

Photo 9 : Nonverbal possessiveness. An older sibling holds a plastic bottle up and away from a toddler so the toddler is not able to reach it.

Photo 10 : Nonverbal possessiveness. Now the older sibling holds the plastic bottle behind her back as the toddler continues trying to reach it.

Photo 11 : Nonverbal possessiveness. The older sibling has now placed the plastic bottle under her armpit to ensure the toddler can not reach it.

Photo 12 : An older sibling teaching a toddler how to play a ball game.

Photo 13 : Talk with demonstration. An older sibling uses talk with demonstration to show a toddler how he should kick a ball.

Photo 14 : Talk with demonstration. An older sibling uses talk with demonstration while teaching a toddler how to dance

3.7.1.4 Discourse variables as per assumptions of the study

The discourse variables were further grouped into three categories according to the assumption of the study that they fell under. The three categories were support or help, manipulation and negative behaviour. Some discourse variables occurred very rarely therefore were not included in the categories. These included praise which occurred only a total of three times and task simplification which occurred only once.

In the negative behaviours category, all measures that were viewed as having been used by the older siblings to handle the toddlers in a cruel, unkind or unfair way were included whereas the manipulation category included all variables the older siblings used to influence the toddlers in order to get the toddlers to behave in certain ways. Help or support category on the other hand included all variables the older siblings used in order to facilitate what the toddlers were doing or saying. A detailed presentation of the variables included in each of the three categories is given in Table 2.

Table 2

Discourse Variables as Per Study Assumptions

Help or support	Manipulation	Negative behaviour
Descriptions/Explanations	Commands	Verbal aggression
Talk with demonstration	Feedback	Nonverbal aggression
Guiding toddlers' body		Verbal possessiveness
		Nonverbal possessiveness

3.8 Statistical analysis

The quantitative data from the interview schedule were coded and data files prepared for computer analysis using Nie, Stein & Bent's (1975) Statistical Package for the Social Sciences (SPSS) while a content analysis was done of the qualitative data.

After the teaching episodes in the video tapes were extracted, they were coded and this data were fed into the Excel software package then converted to SPSS data for analysis. Analysis of variance (ANOVA) and t-test were used to compare how the older siblings of different ages interacted with the toddlers. However, before the ANOVA and t-test were performed, the overall time each older sibling spent interacting with a toddler was controlled for and to do this, frequency counts were taken of each of the measures and then divided by the amount of time each older sibling spent interacting with a toddler. ANOVA was then performed and where significant differences were present, t-tests were performed to determine the degree and direction of the differences.

Dividing the discourse variables by time spent in interactions ensured differences that may have occurred due to variations in time spent in interactions were eliminated. No differences across the age groups in time spent in teaching were revealed, $F(2,61) = 2.77$, $p = .071$. Time spent in interaction was the denominator of all the discourse measures of the study and this non significant difference made analysis and interpretation of the discourse variables easy because discussion of the results focused on the dependent measures.

The results obtained were then multiplied by 30. A multiplication by 30 was done because the data had been entered into a data sheet which had been subdivided into ten second intervals. While six of these ten second intervals would add up to 60 seconds, multiplying the ten second intervals by 30 would result in 300 seconds. Scores of interactions taking place over a five minute span were easier to interpret as opposed to those of interactions taking place each minute since the scores of five minute interactions were higher.

Frequencies obtained therefore reflected the frequencies of the interactions taking place within a span of five minutes. This in effect meant the means obtained once the ANOVA and t-tests were performed would be of interactions occurring over an interval of five minutes. Three groups were compared. These were the three and a half to five year olds (n = 30), six to seven year olds (n = 15) and eight to eleven and a half year olds (n = 22). Age group differences were obtained in some of the discourse variables when ANOVA and t-test were performed. However, there were no effects for gender.

3.9 Reliability

To ensure reliability, coding of the videotaped sessions was first conducted by the researcher and a research assistant unaware of the hypotheses was requested to code 10% of the videotapes to check on inter-rater agreement. Inter-rater agreement assessed by percentage agreement was 84%.

CHAPTER IV
RESULTS

4.1 Item analysis of the interview schedule

The interview schedule provided some background information on the families involved in the study including information on the social context of care giving. The toddlers' mothers reported relatives living in the same homestead as being involved in care giving with grandmothers being mentioned most frequently as providing assistance. Older siblings were also reported to play a significant role since the second largest proportion of the mothers' responses that is 25 % of the responses referred to older siblings as providing assistance. The toddlers' mothers also reported that the older siblings played with the toddlers during caretaking. A more detailed description of the relatives assisting in caretaking is provided in Table 3.

Table 3

Individuals Assisting in Caretaking

Individual	Percent of mothers' responses
Grandmothers	35.4
Older siblings	25
Aunts	16.7
Fathers	12.5
Grandfathers	8.3
None as mother is sole caretaker	2.1
Total	100

When asked what they understood by the term teaching, more than half the mothers' responses that is, 59.46% were that it was making more intelligent or enlightening. Other responses included the opinion that it was taking a child to school and that teaching involved providing information about life in general. A more detailed description of the mothers' views on teaching is provided in Table 4.

Table 4

Toddlers Mothers' Views on Meaning of Teaching

View	Percent of mothers' responses
Enlightening or making more intelligent	59.5
Taking a child to school	16.2
Providing information about life in general	16.2
Advising	5.4
No response	2.7
Total	100

Many of the mothers (26.5%) also believed children should start being taught when they are four years old. A breakdown of the ages mothers believed children should start being taught is displayed in Table 5 and the various reasons given by the mothers for believing a certain age was appropriate to begin teaching are displayed in Table 6. The mothers provided various responses but most mothers appeared to believe the age they thought a child was intelligent or could understand things was the appropriate age for teaching to begin. All the responses the toddlers' mothers gave are displayed in Table 6. The responses are more than 34 which was the number of the toddlers' mothers as some mothers provided more than one response.

Data obtained from the interview schedule therefore not only provided background information on the families but also information on caretaking of the toddlers including information as to which relatives assisted the mothers in taking care of the toddlers. The greatest percent of responses given by the toddlers' mothers mentioned grandmothers and older siblings as providing assistance in caretaking. Data in the interview schedule also revealed that the toddlers' mothers had varying opinions as to what the term teaching meant with many of the mothers saying they understood the term meant making more intelligent or enlightening. Many of the mothers also believed four years was the most appropriate age at which to start teaching children and they also provided various reasons as to why they thought certain ages were appropriate to begin teaching. Therefore, apart from providing background information on the families, the interview schedule also provided information on the toddlers mothers' views.

Table 5

Toddlers Mothers' Views on When Teaching Should Begin

Age in years	Number of mothers	Percent of mothers
From birth	6	17.6
One	3	8.8
Two	5	14.7
Three	3	8.8
Four	9	26.5
Five	7	20.6
Six years and above	1	2.9
Total	34	100

4.2 Statistical analysis of videotape data

4.2.1 Older siblings' support for the toddlers

Analysis of variance was performed for the discourse variables deemed to have reflected instances of older siblings supporting or helping the toddlers. These variables included descriptions and explanations, talk with demonstration and guiding the toddlers' body. The results were in the expected direction with the mean scores showing that older children offered more support to the toddlers than younger children.

Although no significant differences across the age groups were reflected $F(2,61) = 1.08$, $p = 0.346$, when ANOVA was performed for the descriptions and explanations category, the mean scores were in the expected direction with the eight to eleven and a half year olds having higher mean scores (M = 3.723) than the six to seven year olds (M = 2.656) and three and a half to five year olds (M = 2.318).

In talk with demonstration, the eight to eleven and a half year olds had higher mean scores (M = 0.257) than the six to seven year olds (M = 0.190) and the three and a half to five year olds (M = 0.125) although there were no significant differences between the groups $F(2,61) = 0.70$, $p = 0.501$.

Table 6

Toddlers Mothers' Reasons as to Age When Teaching Should Begin

Age in years	Reason	Frequency
From Birth	To make the child more intelligent	2
	Children already understand at this age	4
One	Children should be taught even before joining school	2
	Children should be corrected while young	1
Two	Children can understand at this age	4
	Children should be taught even before joining school	2
Three	Children can understand at this age	1
	Children can be taken to nursery school at this age	2
Four	Children are intelligent at this age	2
	Children can be taken to school at this age	8
	Children can take care of themselves at this age	2
Five	Children are intelligent at this age	1
	Children can be taken to school at this age	5
	So the child can complete school while still young	1
Six and above	Children are intelligent at this age	1
	Total	38

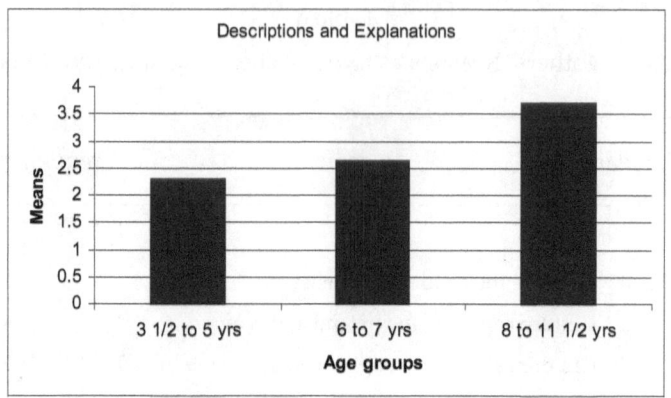

Figure 2 Means of descriptions and explanations by age group

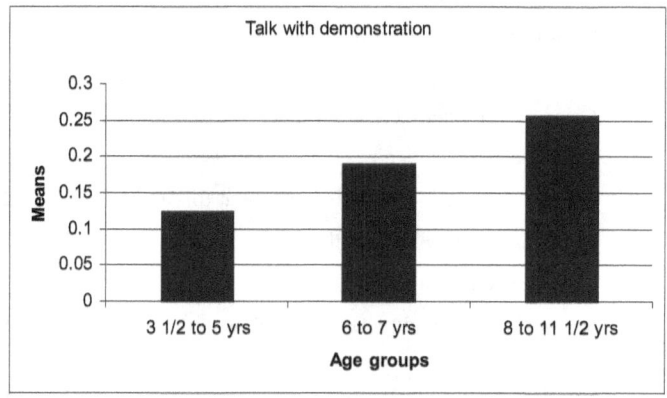

Figure 3 Means of talk with demonstration by age group

There were also no significant differences for guiding the toddlers' body, $F(2,61) = 0.91$, $p = 0.407$ but the older children, that is eight to eleven and a half year olds (M = 0.068) had higher mean scores than the six to seven year olds (M = 0.016) and three and a half to five year olds (M = 0.005).

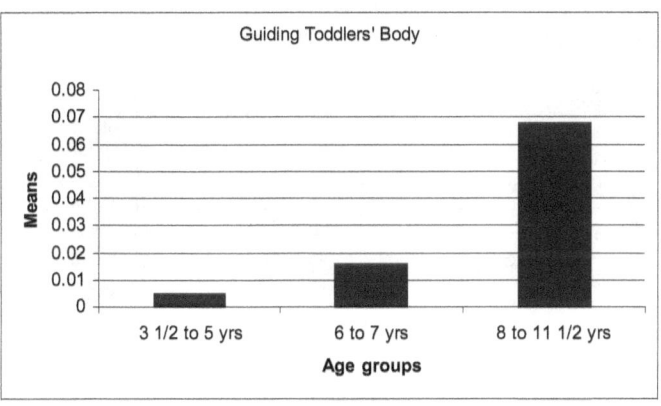

Figure 4 Means of guiding toddlers' body by age group

4.2.2 Older siblings' manipulation of the toddlers

Analysis of variance was performed for the discourse variables deemed to have reflected instances of older siblings manipulating the toddlers. These variables included commands and feedback.

ANOVA revealed a significant relation between the factor of age and commands, $F(2,61) = 25.43$, $p < .05$. This significant result was further analysed by Bonferroni t-test to find specific inter-group differences. There was a significant difference between the youngest age group, the three and a half to five year olds ($M = 5.167$) and the oldest age group, the eight to eleven and a half year olds ($M = 15.494$), $t(27) = -6.33$, $p < .05$. T-test also revealed a significant difference between the six to seven year olds ($M = 8.175$) and the eight to eleven and a half year olds ($M = 15.494$), $t(34) = -3.46$, $p < .05$. However, although the results were in the expected direction with the older children having higher means, the three and a half to five year olds ($M = 5.167$) did not differ significantly from the six to seven year olds ($M = 8.175$), $t(19) = -1.90$, $p = 0.07$.

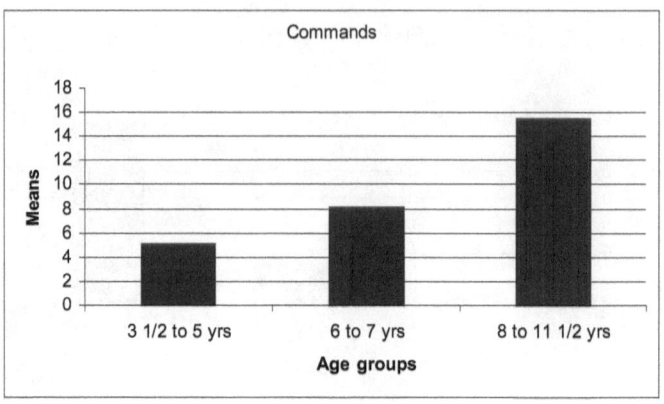

Figure 5 Means of commands by age group

There were significant relations between the factors of age and feedback, $F(2,61) = 4.52$, $p < .05$. Bonferroni t-tests revealed a significant difference between the three and a half to five year olds ($M = 0.011$) and the eight to eleven and a half year olds ($M = 0.268$), $t(50) = -2.39$, $p < .05$. There were however no significant differences between the six to seven year olds ($M = 0.05$) and the eight to eleven and a half year olds ($M = 0.268$), $t(35) = -1.40$, $p = 0.17$ nor was there any significant difference between the three and a half to five year olds ($M = 0.011$) and the six to seven year olds ($M = 0.05$), $t(43) = -1.38$, $p = 0.17$ although the older children had higher mean scores.

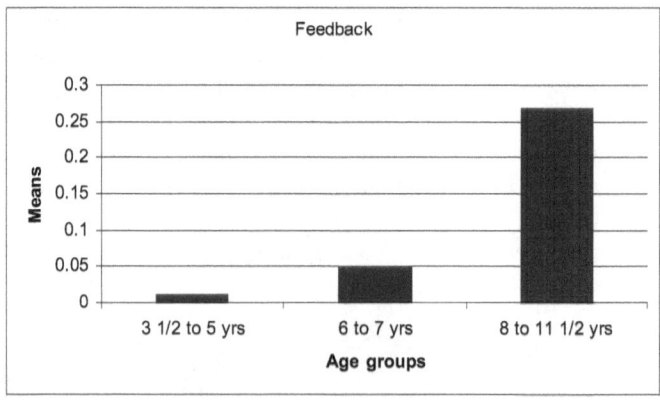

Figure 6 Means of feedback by age group

4.2.3 Older siblings' negative behaviour

Verbal aggression, nonverbal aggression, verbal possessiveness and nonverbal possessiveness were included under negative behaviour. ANOVA revealed a significant difference for the factor of age and verbal aggression, $F(2,61) = 5.47$, $p < .05$. Further analysis using t-test showed a significant difference between the three and a half to five year olds ($M = 0.242$) and eight to eleven and a half year olds ($M = 0.045$), $t(35) = 3.21$, $p < .05$. There was also a significant difference between the three and a half to five year olds ($M = 0.242$) and the six to seven year olds ($M = 0.061$), $t(42) = 2.67$, $p < .05$. However, there was no significant difference between the six to seven year olds ($M = 0.061$) and the eight to eleven and a half year olds ($M = 0.045$), $t(22) = 0.41$, $p = 0.69$.

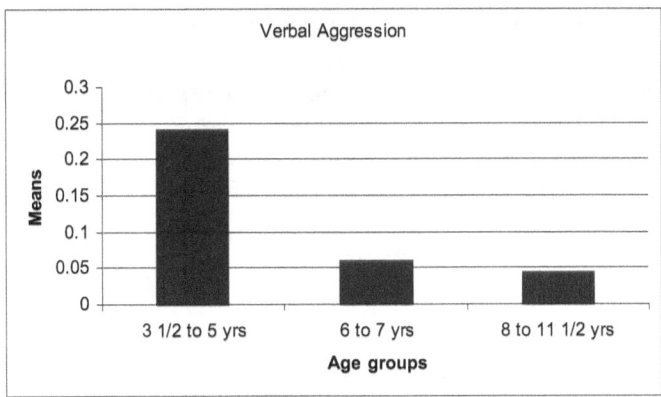

Figure 7 Means of verbal aggression by age group

In the nonverbal aggression category, the youngest children that is the three and a half to five year olds had a higher mean score ($M = 0.275$) than the six to seven year olds ($M = 0.085$) and eight to nine year olds ($M = 0.013$). However, although the results were in the expected direction, ANOVA did not reveal any significant differences $F(2,61) = 1.96$, $p = 0.15$.

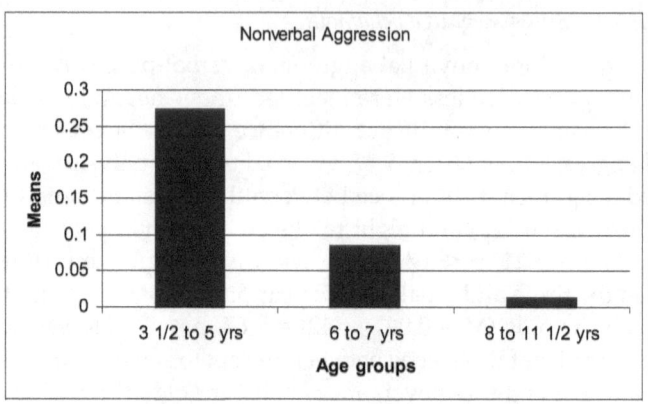

Figure 8 Means of nonverbal aggression by age group

In verbal possessiveness, the results were in the expected direction with the younger children that is the three and a half to five year olds (M = 0.162) having higher mean scores than the older ones that is, the six to seven (M = 0.148) and the eight to eleven and a half year olds (M = 0.059). However, ANOVA did not reveal any significant differences, $F(2,61) = 0.46$, $p = 0.63$.

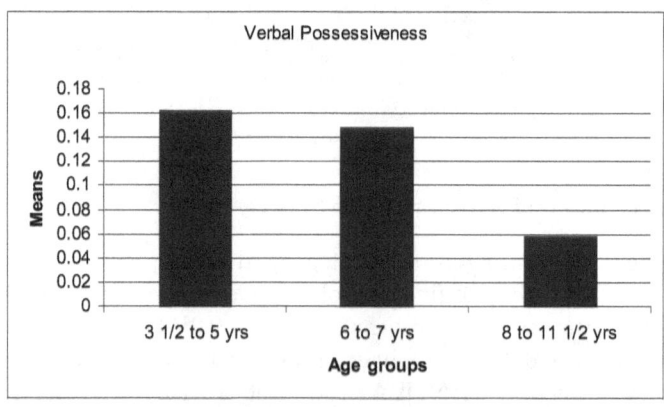

Figure 9 Means of verbal possessiveness by age group

The three and a half to five year olds also had a higher mean score (M = 1.584) than the six to seven year olds (M = 0.341) and eight to eleven and a half year olds (M = 0.234) in the nonverbal possessiveness category. However, although younger children had higher mean scores, ANOVA did not reveal any significant differences, F(2,61) = 0.89, p = 0.42.

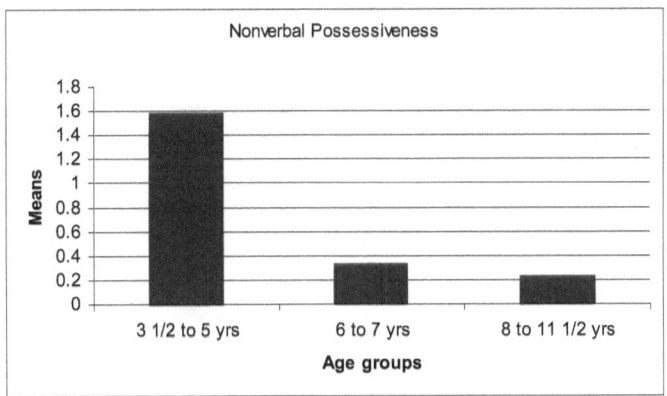

Figure 10 Means of nonverbal possessiveness by age group

4.2.4 Older siblings' use of verbal and nonverbal discourse variables

In order to obtain an overview of the trend in which the children in the different age groups used the discourse variables, the verbal and the nonverbal discourse variables were also added up. Two categories were therefore formed that is, one of the verbal discourse variables and another of the nonverbal discourse variables. The variables were therefore included under either of the two categories depending on which category they fell under except for talk with demonstration which could not be included in either of the categories as it was both verbal and nonverbal.

The variables included under the verbal discourse variables category were descriptions and explanations, commands, feedback, verbal aggression and verbal possessiveness. Although praise was one of the verbal discourse variables in this study, it was not included because as had been stated earlier on, it occurred only a total of three times in all the data collected.

An analysis of variance was then performed on the verbal discourse variables and it revealed a significant difference for the factor of age, $F(2,61) = 17.45$, $p < .05$. This significant result was further analysed by Bonferroni t-test to find specific inter-group differences. There was a significant difference between the three and a half to five year olds (M = 7.890) and the eight to eleven and a half year olds (M = 19.321), $t(35) = -5.87$, $p < .05$. T-test also revealed a significant difference between the six to seven year olds (M = 11.039) and the eight to eleven and a half year olds (M = 19.321), $t(30) = -3.13$, $p < .05$. However, although the results were in the expected direction with the older children having higher means, the three and a half to five year olds (M = 7.890) did not differ significantly from the six to seven year olds (M = 11.039), $t(21) = -1.38$, $p = 0.18$.

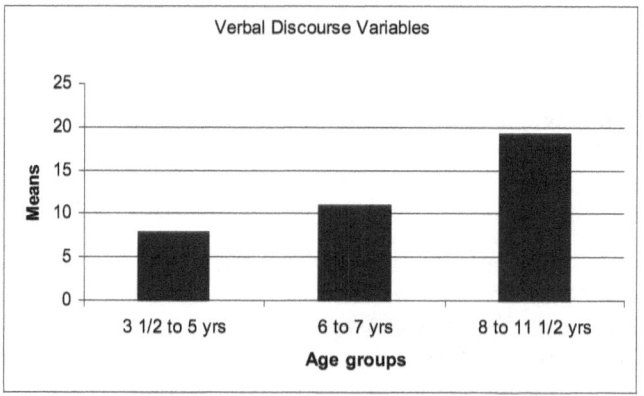

Figure 11 Means of verbal discourse variables by age group

Analysis of variance was also performed on the nonverbal discourse variables. The nonverbal discourse variables included in this category were, guiding the toddlers' body, nonverbal possessiveness and nonverbal aggressiveness. Task simplification was not included because as stated earlier on, it only occurred once in all the data collected. ANOVA however did not reveal a significant difference for the factor of age and the nonverbal discourse variables, F(2,61) = 1.13, *p* = 0.329. The results however were in the expected direction with the mean scores showing that younger children used more nonverbal discourse variables than older children. The three and a half to five year olds had higher mean scores (M = 1.864) than the six to seven year olds (M = 0.441) and the eight to eleven and a half year olds (M = 0.316). Younger children therefore seemed to engage in more nonverbal interactions with the toddlers than older children.

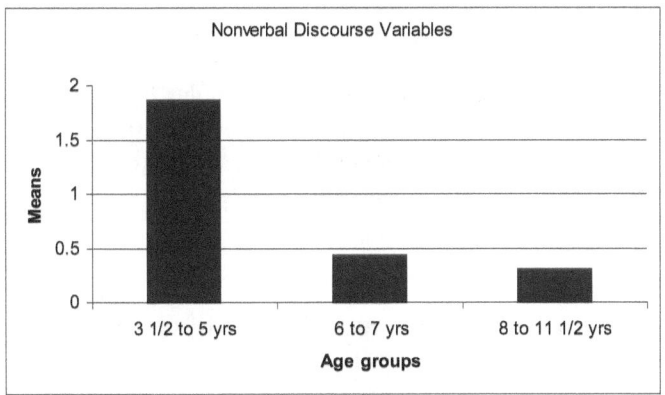

Figure 12 Means of nonverbal discourse variables by age group

4.3 Qualitative data analysis of videotape data

As has just been discussed above, there were significant relationships between age group and three of the discourse variables, namely commands, feedback and verbal aggression. This section contains examples which help illustrate the quantitative results. The examples included in this section contain instances when older siblings from the different age groups used some of the discourse variables. The nonverbal information has been presented in double parentheses.

Example 1: Age 9. This example particularly demonstrates use of commands, descriptions, task simplification and feedback by an older sibling from the oldest age group that is from the eight to eleven and a half year olds age group. A nine year old boy called Kamau is interacting with his two year old sister and the interaction takes place as the children feed some cows.

Kamau: ((To Toddler))

    Go and get leaves for the cow

((Kamau and the Toddler walk towards the cow sheds. The Toddler picks a handful of grass from a sack nearby and takes it to the cows then she starts walking back towards Kamau))

Toddler: ((To Kamau))

    They have finished

((Kamau breaks a maize stalk into two smaller bits and gives the toddler the smaller bit of maize stalk to take to the cows. The Toddler walks back to the cows and starts feeding them. Some stalks have fallen on the ground))

Kamau: ((To Toddler))

    And also those ones (referring to the stalks that have fallen on the ground)

((The Toddler picks the stalks on the ground and feeds them to the cows then she runs back to Kamau))

Kamau: ((To Toddler))

    Pick some more

((The Toddler picks some more grass from the sack))

Toddler: ((To Kamau))

    They have finished

Kamau: ((To Toddler))

    Take more

((Kamau holds the mouth of the sack so that the Toddler can take more grass out of the sack. The Toddler walks to the cows holding grass in both hands. She starts singing as she feeds the cows))

Toddler: ((To the cows))

Kamau: And you! And you! And you!
((To Toddler))
Come

The hierarchical organisation clearly puts Kamau as the older child in charge here. In this section, he gives commands such as asking the toddler to get leaves for the cows and he also tells her to pick some maize stalks that have fallen on the ground and feed them to the cows. As the older child, Kamau seems to realise the toddler has limited abilities and instead of giving her a long maize stalk, breaks it into smaller bits which she can easily handle. In doing this, he actually simplifies a task for the toddler. In the following section, Kamau uses commands, a description and feedback while interacting with the toddler.

((The Toddler runs back to Kamau. The Toddler wants to take more grass out of the sack but Kamau has already tied the mouth of the sack))

Kamau: ((To Toddler))
We won't feed them anymore

((The Toddler walks away from Kamau. She starts staring into the camera then turns and looks at Kamau who is still standing next to the sack of grass))

Toddler: ((To Kamau))
Let us go

Kamau: ((To Toddler))
Where?

((The Toddler starts biting the seam of her blouse, says something inaudible then walks towards Kamau))

Toddler: ((To Kamau))
Kamau

((The children's mother who is in the kitchen, calls Kamau))

Mum: ((From the background to Kamau))
Kamau, give them (cows) the grass

((Kamau opens the sack again. The children's mother says something inaudible))

Kamau: ((To Mum))

    What?

((Kamau takes some grass out of the sack and gives it to the Toddler))

Kamau: ((To the Toddler))

    Go and give them (cows)

((The Toddler takes the grass and gives it to the cows then she walks back extending her hand towards Kamau))

Toddler: ((To Kamau))

    Bring! Bring!

((The Toddler takes more grass from Kamau and walks back to feed the cows))

Kamau: ((To Toddler))

    Give the big one (cow)

Toddler: ((To Kamau))

    Yes

((The Toddler starts walking towards a cow))

Kamau: ((To Toddler))

    Not that one

Toddler: ((To Kamau))

    What?

((Kamau points to another cow))

Kamau: ((To Toddler))

    That one

Toddler: ((To Kamau))

    That one?

((The Toddler walks towards the cow Kamau pointed at and starts giving it some of the grass))

Kamau: ((To Toddler))

    Give it all (the grass)

((The Toddler continues giving the grass to the cow in bits until she has given it all the grass))

In the interaction section presented above, it is clear that Kamau as the older child is in charge. He decides what is to be done for example he decides that the children will not feed the cows anymore and he uses a description of an anticipated activity to state this fact. Kamau also issues commands for example he tells the toddler to go and give the cows some grass, tells the toddler which cow to feed and also tells her to give a cow all the grass. Kamau further provides feedback to the toddlers' actions by informing her that she is feeding the wrong cow. In the following and last section of this example, Kamau uses another description and also issues commands to the toddler.

((The Toddler turns and starts walking towards Kamau))

Toddler: ((To Kamau))

    It has finished

Kamau: ((To Toddler))

    Come. We will now cut some firewood

((Kamau walks to the side of the cowshed and the Toddler follows him. Kamau bends over and is partially out of view. He can be seen handing the Toddler a stick))

Kamau: ((To Toddler))

    Break the firewood

((The Toddler stands near him holding the stick))

Kamau: ((To Toddler))

    Break it!

((The Toddler moves closer to Kamau and starts watching him. Kamau is still bending over and is now out of view))

Toddler: ((To Kamau))

    Let us go! Let us go!

((Kamau stands up straight and can now be clearly seen))

Kamau: ((To Toddler))

Okay, let us go

((The Toddler starts walking to the foreground with Kamau following her. Both children are carrying sticks in their hands. The Toddler starts staring into the camera))

In this section Kamau decides what will be done and uses a description to tell of the next activity that the children will undertake which is cutting firewood. Kamau is still in charge in this section and also gives a command to the toddler by telling her to break the firewood. In fact, it is clear from the whole of example one that the hierarchical organisation clearly puts the older child in charge throughout the interaction. The same trend of the older sibling being in charge can also be seen in the next example where a six year old and a ten year old older sibling interact with a toddler.

Example 2: Age 6 and 10. This example particularly demonstrates use of commands, nonverbal aggression, nonverbal possessiveness and verbal possessiveness by a six year old and also use of commands, praise, descriptions and nonverbal aggression by a ten year old. In this example six year old Maurine, ten year old Njeri and three and a half year old Karega interact with Lucy, the toddler. Also at the scene is a baby called Rachel who is about nine months old. The children are playing with a plastic bottle and later play school.

((The children are standing or sitting near a granary in the homestead. The baby is crying and Njeri is holding her and trying to calm her down. The Toddler is holding a plastic bottle. Maurine grabs the bottle from the Toddler))

Maurine: ((To Toddler))

Bring my item!

((Although Maurine manages to grab the bottle from the Toddler, the Toddler scratches her face. Maurine puts the mouth of the bottle into her own mouth. The Toddler screams and starts reaching out for the bottle. Maurine holds the bottle high above so that the Toddler can not reach it. The Toddler continues screaming and crying. Maurine runs to the right and stands a few steps away from the Toddler))

Maurine: ((To Toddler))

It is mine! It is mine!

((Maurine puts the mouth of the bottle into her mouth again and starts drinking some water that is in the bottle. The Toddler continues screaming and crying))

In this section Maurine as the older child is clearly in charge. However, as the older child she uses her position and physical strength to direct negative behaviour towards the toddler for example she is nonverbally aggressive and grabs a bottle from the toddler. Maurine is also verbally possessive and refers to the bottle as her own. She also displays nonverbal possessiveness when she refuses to share a bottle with the toddler and holds it high up above her head so the toddler can not reach it. In the next section, Njeri also displays some negative behaviour but she also gives some praise, issues some commands and uses descriptions.

((Maurine stops drinking from the bottle and walks to Karega. Karega is standing next to Njeri who is holding the baby in her arms))

Maurine: ((To Karega))

Let me beat you

((Maurine holds Karega's hand and uses the bottle to hit Karega's palm lightly. She then takes the bottle and puts its mouth in her own mouth, sucks from it briefly then puts the mouth of the bottle in the baby's mouth. The Toddler has stopped crying and is watching Njeri who is holding the baby. Njeri starts putting the baby on the ground))

Njeri: ((To baby))

Stay here with the bottle

((The baby starts crying again. Maurine has put the mouth of the bottle in her own mouth again and is sucking from the bottle. Njeri reaches out, takes the bottle from Maurine and gives it to the baby who she has now placed on the ground. Njeri then picks a stick from the ground))

Njeri: ((To Toddler, Maurine and Karega))

Go and get your books! Come here!

Maurine: ((To Njeri))

I don't want (to play)

((The Toddler has walked to the baby and taken the bottle from the baby. The baby starts crying again. Karega is running away from the scene. Njeri calls her))

Njeri: ((To Karega))

Karega come!

Karega: ((To Njeri))

I am going to get my books

Njeri: ((To Karega))

Why did you come to class without books?

Njeri: ((To Toddler))

Come here Lucy!

Njeri: ((To Karega))

When you come to this classroom I will beat you!

((The Toddler is now using the bottle to hit the palm of her hand lightly. She walks towards Karega and pulls at her hand))

Toddler: ((To Karega))

Bring I beat you!

((Karega pulls her hand away and runs away from the scene. The baby is still crying))

Njeri: ((To the baby))

Keep quiet

((Njeri walks to the Toddler and grabs the bottle from the Toddler's hands))

Njeri: ((To Toddler))

You! Bring!

((Njeri gives the bottle to the baby then walks to Maurine and tries to take her hand))

Njeri: ((To Maurine))

Bring Maurine

Maurine: ((To Njeri))

I don't want to (play)

Njeri: ((To Maurine))

You want to (play)! You want to!

((Njeri pulls Maurine's hand and starts hitting her lightly with the stick that she is holding))

Maurine: ((To Njeri))

I don't want to (play)

Njeri: ((To Maurine))

You want to (play)! You want to!

((The Toddler has been watching the older girls and is still watching them. Njeri counts up to six as she hits Maurine's palm lightly))

Njeri: ((To Maurine))

One, two, three, four, five, six. I have beaten you six times. You still have four left

((Njeri continues to use the stick to hit Maurine lightly on various parts of her body))

Njeri: ((To Maurine))

Seven, eight, nine and one more. Bring your hand! Bring your hand!

((Njeri is finally able to hit Maurine's palm. Maurine also hits Njeri lightly on her back))

Njeri: ((To Maurine))

Ten! Now go and get your books! Go and get your books! See Karega went away! When she comes back I will also beat her!

((The Toddler is still watching the older girls))

Njeri: ((To Toddler))

Lucy! Come here! Come I beat you!

((The Toddler walks towards Njeri and Njeri takes her hand))

Njeri: ((To Maurine))

Lucy is not like you (Maurine and Karega). You (Maurine and Karega) are bad!

Njeri as the oldest child is clearly in charge. She issues commands to the younger children including the toddler for example she tells the younger children to go and get their books and she also tells the toddler to walk towards her. Njeri however like Maurine uses her position and physical strength to direct negative behaviour towards the toddler for example she displays nonverbally aggressive behaviour when she grabs a bottle from the toddler. Although Njeri is nonverbally aggressive, she also praises the toddler by saying that the toddler is not like the other bad older siblings because the toddler has followed her instructions. In the next section, Njeri continues to interact with the toddler and uses a command, a description and is nonverbally aggressive towards the toddler.

((Njeri is now holding the Toddler's hand but the Toddler has held her hand in a fist))

Njeri: ((To Toddler))

Don't fold your fingers!

((The Toddler stretches out her fingers so that her palm is facing upwards. The baby starts crying and Maurine goes to pick her up. Njeri uses the stick to hit the Toddler's palm lightly. Njeri is counting as she hits the Toddler's palm))

Njeri: ((To Toddler))

One!

((The Toddler tries to pull her palm away but Njeri is still holding her wrist))

Njeri: ((To Toddler))

Two!

((The Toddler makes a hissing sound with her mouth and tries to pull her palm away again but Njeri is still holding her wrist (*The Toddler appears to be feeling pain when Njeri hits her with the stick*). Njeri continues to hold the Toddler's wrist))

Njeri: ((To Maurine and the Toddler))

I have beaten Lucy twice

((Njeri gets ready to hit the Toddler a third time but the Toddler continues to pull her hand away. The Toddler is finally able to pull her hand away))

Njeri: ((To Maurine and the Toddler))

God! Lucy is not part of our game!

((The Toddler stands to the left of Njeri and continues to watch the older children. Maurine is now holding the baby and standing next to Njeri. The baby keeps on crying and sometimes keeping quiet))

Njeri in this section issues a command when she tells the toddler not to fold her fingers. She is also nonverbally aggressive as she continues hitting the toddler's palm even when the toddler shows that she is clearly feeling pain. Njeri also uses descriptions for example she says what she has just done after she lightly hits the toddlers' palm and she also says that the toddler is not part of the game.

Just like in the first example, the older children are clearly in charge here with Njeri who is the oldest taking charge more than the other children while Karega who is the youngest of the older siblings does not interact a lot with the toddler. This hierarchical ordering can also be seen in the next example where a seven year old sibling interacts with a toddler.

Example 3: Age 7. This example particularly demonstrates use of descriptions, talk with demonstration, commands and nonverbal aggression by a seven year old older sibling. Ciru a seven year old girl is interacting with her two year old cousin Njoroge. Also at the scene are four year old Wanjiku and three and a half year old Wainaina who however do not interact a lot with the toddler in this section. The children are playing a game where Ciru tries to catch them.

((The Toddler and his siblings are standing in a space between the houses in the compound. The Toddler's mother and an aunt are seated to the right and Ciru is trying to place a bench on the ground near them then sit on it. The Toddler and Wainaina are running up to Ciru then running away from her when she tries to touch them. Ciru is now seated on the bench. The Toddler and Wainaina are standing in front of Ciru))

Ciru: ((To Toddler and Wainaina))

I am the one who is chasing you! I will hit you like *"peea!"* (*"peea"* has no meaning. It is just a sound Ciru makes supposedly to emphasise the manner in which she will catch the other two children)

((Ciru raises her hands to show how she will catch the two children. The Toddler and Wainaina raise their legs as if to kick Ciru but do not kick her))

Toddler: ((To Ciru))

Peea!

((Ciru leans forward while still seated on the bench. The Toddler and Wainaina laugh and run away from her. Wanjiku has also just joined in the game and she also runs away laughing. The children continue running towards Ciru and away from her every time she tries to catch them))

Toddler: ((To Ciru))

A person! A person!

((Ciru manages to catch the Toddler then lets go of him. Wanjiku pushes the Toddler towards Ciru. Ciru pulls the Toddler and starts tickling him. The Toddler sits on the ground and laughs. Ciru is still pulling and tickling him))

Ciru: ((To Toddler))

I have caught you Njoroge!

Ciru as the oldest child is clearly in charge. She uses a description when she talks of how she is the one chasing the other children and also uses a description when she talks of what has just happened after catching the toddler. She also uses talk with demonstration in this section when she raises her hands and at the same time describes how she will catch the other children. In the following section, Ciru continues to interact with the toddler and uses commands and nonverbal aggression during the interaction.

((The Toddler gets up and walks towards his mother and aunt who are seated to the right then he walks a few steps to the left and is closer to Ciru. Ciru starts tickling him again. The Toddler laughs and moves away from her))

Ciru: ((To Toddler))

Should I drink this porridge?

((Ciru is referring to the Toddler's cup of porridge that is lying on the ground near the Toddler's mother. The Toddler looks at her then starts watching Wanjiku and Wainaina who are pulling each other in the foreground. Wanjiku and Wainaina walk towards Ciru and stand in front of her. Wanjiku is pulling Wainaina))

Wanjiku: ((To Ciru))

Here is one! Here is one!

((Wainaina starts screaming))

Ciru: ((To Wanjiku))

Stop pulling him (Wainaina)! Stop pulling him!

((Ciru turns and looks at the Toddler))

Ciru: ((To Toddler))

Come and drink your porridge

Wanjiku: ((To Ciru))

Here I am! Here I am!

((Ciru turns around and tries to catch Wanjiku while still seated on the bench. Wanjiku runs away laughing. The Toddler has now moved closer to Ciru and picked up the cup of porridge. Ciru turns towards him and grabs the cup from him))

Ciru: ((To Toddler))

Bring!

((Ciru puts the cup against her lips and starts drinking from it. The Toddler starts running around and crying loudly))

Ciru as the oldest child is again clearly in charge. She issues a command to the toddler by telling him to go and drink his porridge and also tells him to bring the cup of porridge. However, Ciru also uses her position and physical strength as the older child to display nonverbal aggression towards the toddler when she grabs the cup of porridge from him.

Just like in the first two examples, the older child is clearly in charge here with Ciru who is older taking charge over the toddler. This hierarchical ordering can also be seen in the next example where a five year old sibling interacts with a toddler.

Example 4: Age 5. This example particularly demonstrates an older sibling from the youngest age group using commands and verbal aggression while interacting with a toddler. Muracie the five year old boy interacts with his two year old sister Wambui as the children play with a radio. Mburu the children's four year old cousin is also at the scene but he does not interact with the toddler in this section.

((The children are inside one of the houses in the homestead but are right next to the door so they are clearly visible to the people who are outside in the compound. Muracie is seated on a bench and the toddler is standing next to him. The children are fiddling with a radio while Mburu is seated nearby on a bench and is eating some sugarcane.))

Muracie: ((Shouts at the toddler))

    Leave the radio alone!

((The Toddler starts pulling at Muracie's hand))

Muracie: ((Shouts at the toddler))

    Aaah! (sound showing frustration)

((Muracie pulls his hand away and puts it back on the radio. The Toddler pulls again at his hand))

Muracie: ((To Toddler))

    Stop!

((The Toddler continues pulling at Muracie and when he pulls away, she starts hitting him lightly on the shoulders and chest))

Muracie: ((To no one in particular in a complaining voice))

    This one (referring to the Toddler)!

Muracie: ((To Toddler))

    I will hit you!

((The Toddler continues touching the radio. A song starts being played on the radio and Muracie and the Toddler start singing along then stop singing when the radio presenter interrupts the song. They start examining the radio once more))

Just like in the other three examples, Muracie as the oldest child is clearly in charge however he uses his position to direct negative behaviour in the form of verbal aggression towards the toddler. He shouts at the toddler and tells her to stop touching the radio and also to stop pulling at his hand. Muracie even goes to the extent of threatening the toddler that he will hit her in order to get her to do his bidding.

4.4 Summary of the statistical and qualitative analysis

The qualitative data analysis examples provided above help to better illustrate the quantitative results presented earlier. It is clear from the examples that all the children demonstrated a similar pattern of behaviour with children showing abilities according to age and social status.

Older children tended to use descriptions and explanations, talk with demonstration and guiding of the toddlers' bodies more than younger children. The oldest children that is the eight to eleven and a half year olds also gave significantly more commands than the youngest children that is the three and a half to five year olds. The oldest children also gave significantly more commands than the middle age group that is, they gave more commands than the six to seven year olds.

There was also a significant difference between the youngest and oldest children in terms of the amount of feedback they gave with the oldest children giving significantly more feedback than the youngest children. The results also revealed a significant difference in verbal aggression with the youngest children using significantly more verbal aggression than the oldest children and also significantly more verbal aggression than the children in the middle age group that is, the six to seven year olds.

The youngest children also displayed more nonverbal aggression than the older children in the other two age groups although no significant differences were revealed in this category. The same trend was also seen in the possessiveness category with the youngest children being more verbally and nonverbally possessive than the older children in the other two age groups although again there were no significant differences between the age groups.

In general, older children used more verbal discourse variables than younger children. Specifically, there was a significant difference in the amount of verbal discourse variables used by the three and a half to five year olds and the eight to eleven and a half year olds. There was also a significant difference between the six to seven year olds and the eight to eleven and a half year olds with the older children using significantly more verbal discourse variables. However, although the six to seven year olds had higher mean scores, there was no significant difference between this group and the three and a half to five year olds.

The results also revealed that the younger children used more nonverbal discourse variables although the differences were not significant between the age groups. The mean scores showed that the three and a half to five year olds had higher mean scores in use of nonverbal discourse variables than the six to seven year olds and the eight to eleven and a half year olds. The six to seven year olds also used more nonverbal discourse variables than the eight to eleven and a half year olds.

Although there were variations between the age groups, the children also displayed some similarities as they all hardly gave any praise. In the 34 hours of tape, there were only three instances when praise was given. Another similarity was that task simplification was virtually not present as there was only one instance when an older sibling used task simplification. Therefore, although there were differences between the age groups, there were also some similarities between them.

CHAPTER V
DISCUSSION

5.1 Variables of the study

The data presented here have shown the development of children's teaching in its cultural context. Specifically, this study examined the teaching practices of children ages three and a half to eleven and a half as they interacted with their two year old siblings. The results showed that the older siblings demonstrated their abilities according to their age and social status and this is even more evident when each of the variables of the study is examined in turn.

5.1.1 Older siblings' support for the toddlers

The results showed that older children provided more support or help to the toddlers in terms of using descriptions and explanations, talk with demonstration and guiding of the toddlers' bodies. Maynard (1999) had presented similar findings as she also found that older children use more descriptions and explanations, talk with demonstration and guiding of toddlers' bodies.

Although there were no significant differences between the age groups, it was quite clear from the mean scores that the older children were more likely to offer help to the toddlers than younger children. It is probable that the older siblings' willingness to assist their younger siblings may have been due to the realisation that the younger siblings had limited abilities and were therefore trying to help them. This tendency to help is not surprising as previous studies (Abramovitch, Corter & Lando, 1979; Cicerelli, 1975; Dunn, 1983) have shown that older siblings teach their toddler siblings how to solve concrete problems, scaffold and help augment their attention span during play interactions, provide explanations and descriptions, and modify their instructions in accordance with the younger child's performance.

The tendency to provide assistance among the Agikuyu children involved in this study probably stemmed from a sense of duty to help the toddlers. This tendency to help is not unusual as training for responsibility of the older siblings had already started taking place when they were left in charge of the toddlers. The adults in the homesteads were not always in the background and the older siblings knew they were responsible for the toddlers and had to take care of them when the adults were not present. The helping behaviour displayed by the children in this study may be a reflection of the sense of duty to help found in the wider Agikuyu society. However, helping younger members is not the only characteristic of the Agikuyu society. Respect and obedience for elders is another characteristic and this seems to have been socialized by use of commands and feedback by the children in this study that is, by use of manipulation.

5.1.2 Older siblings' manipulation of the toddlers

The data showed that older children gave significantly more commands and feedback than younger children. This is probably because the Agikuyu social organisation and status put the eldest children in charge therefore they had the right to issue more directives to the younger ones. In fact, the mean scores for commands showed that it was the discourse variable used most often by the older siblings.

These results are similar to those of Tomasello and Mannle (1985) who found that older siblings produced more directives than younger siblings. Maynard (1999) also found that commands were the most frequent form of discourse used by Zinacantec children in their teaching interactions. The Zinacantec hierarchical system was actually socialized by parents' and older siblings' use of commands in training younger children. This is also the case among the Agikuyu where younger people are expected to respect and obey their elders and this may be one of the reasons why the older siblings issued many commands to the toddlers.

Individuals in another Kenyan community that is the Gusii were also found to use commands when communicating with their infants (Levine, 2002). In fact, infant directed utterances from all caregivers and at all ages combined showed that 61.4% were commands and after 12 months, negative commands like "stop" and "get away" became more frequent. Directing commands towards younger members in a bid to control their activities therefore seems to be widespread in different communities.

Feedback also seemed to have been used for the same purpose which was to control the activities being undertaken by reinforcing or discouraging the toddlers in the activities they were engaged in. By using feedback, the older siblings were probably socializing the toddlers to respect and obey them since as stated earlier on, obedience and respect for authority are aspects of the hierarchical relationship among the Agikuyu. Younger people are expected to respect their elders (Kenyatta, 1965). Maynard (1999) also found that Zinacantec Maya siblings used feedback during their interactions.

Commands and feedback therefore seem to be widely used and this is in line with the findings of this study where older siblings used commands and feedback when interacting with the toddlers. However, although the older siblings may have used commands and feedback in order to control the state of affairs, they also used other tactics such as displaying negative behaviour in order to get the toddlers to do their bidding.

5.1.3 Older siblings' negative behaviour

This children's display of negative behaviour towards the toddlers is similar to previous findings (Eisenberg & Garvey, 1981) where children's play was sometimes characterised by adverse episodes. The findings of this study were that younger children directed more negative behaviour towards the toddlers. This was especially so in the case of verbal aggression where the younger children displayed significantly more verbal aggression than the older ones. The older children probably displayed less nonverbal aggression because siblings display less physical aggression as they become older (Abramovitch et al., 1986; Felson, 1983; McGuire, et. al, 2000).

The results of this study also indicated that the children in the youngest age group were more possessive with their items than the older children. Jealousy that the toddlers had taken their place as the babies in the families could be one of the reasons why the younger children were reluctant to share with them as research (Yewchuk & Schlosser, 1996) shows siblings can be jealous of each other. It is possible that the younger children were jealous of the toddlers therefore were less likely to display favourable behaviour towards them and hence their refusal to share with them.

Some researchers (McGuire et. al., 2000) argue it is possible that quarrelling over rights and property is a unique and consistent characteristic of the sibling relationship, at least while both children live at home and this is probably why the children were being possessive. The children's possessiveness may be linked to their developing sense of self, social comparison, and positive justice as they deal with ownership and fairness (Damon, 1980; Harter, 1983; Ruble, Boggiano, Feldman, & Loebl, 1980).

The findings on negative behaviour however contrast with those of Rabain-Jamin et al. (2003) who found that Wolof siblings used all kinds of pragmatic skills in order to avoid conflict since they preferred harmony over conflict. Other researchers (West, Pen & Ashleigh, 2002) also argue that individuals are predicted to behave more altruistically and less competitively toward their relatives, because they share a relatively high proportion of their genes. Weisner (1982) also argues that sibling care giving breeds interdependence among siblings that entails the management of conflict to regain and maintain harmony. This may probably explain why the older siblings displayed less negative behaviour. Since they were older, it is probable that with time they had learnt of the need to maintain harmony therefore were less apt to display negative behaviour.

Lack of significant differences in the possessiveness and non-verbal aggression categories may have been partially attributed to interference by adults. The toddlers usually started crying when older children displayed negative behaviour towards them and their crying usually drew the attention of adults in the background. It was only natural for the adults to interfere when the children started fighting over items or when they felt the toddlers were in danger. The researcher could certainly not ask them not to interfere for example when the older children hurt the toddlers such as by hitting or scratching them. Other observational studies of preschool siblings (Ross, et. al., 1996) have also found that parents intervene in as much as 63% of sibling fights and siblings have also cited parental intervention as the most common method of ending sibling fights (McGuire et. al., 2000).

However, even in the categories where the differences were not significant, the trend was the same with the younger children displaying more negative behaviour. A reason for this could be that the children in the youngest age group had probably not yet internalized the social rules governing proper behaviour towards others therefore tended to display more negative behaviour.

5.2 General discussion

The older siblings more advanced skills that were evident across the years of middle childhood were probably due to development of socio-cognitive abilities (Piaget, 1952, 1967) and effects of language development. The more advanced language skills were evident in use of verbal instructions where older children gave significantly more verbal instructions than younger ones that is, the three and a half to five year olds gave the least amount of verbal instructions while the eight to eleven and a half year olds displayed more advanced verbal skills. Other researchers have found that older siblings say more (Dunn & Munn, 1985; Lollis et. al, 1999) and this is obviously due to more advanced verbal skills.

Similar results to those presented here were also obtained in earlier studies (Maynard, 1999) where a positive correlation was found to exist between teacher age, verbal instruction and teacher use of strategies. Older children displayed more advanced skills and this is probably because the youngest age group, that is the three and a half to five year olds had not yet mastered the teaching skills. As suggested by Tomasello et. al, (1993), children in this age group first show evidence of spontaneous efforts to teach or regulate the learning of others. These children may be acquiring the teaching skills at this age but the skills may not yet be sufficient for them to engage their toddler siblings in the same manner that the older children would be able to. The children's teaching skills were therefore developing as they got older. A similar argument is also put forward by Maynard (1999) who found that elements of the adult Zinacantec model of teaching did not develop all at once. Instead, the elements developed sequentially as the children got older. Minnett, et. al. (1983) also found that older children show more teaching skills.

The three and a half to five year olds interaction with the toddlers tended to be nonverbal. In fact, this age group had the highest mean scores in use of the nonverbal discourse variables. It is probable that this age group used more nonverbal discourse variables as their use of verbal discourse variables reduced. These results are similar to those of Maynard (1999) who found that the youngest children gave the least amount of verbal instruction and their teaching behaviour was mostly nonverbal.

The fact that there was virtually no praise is not a surprise as this is characteristic of the Agikuyu social interactions. The older siblings were probably just reflecting the society's mode of social interaction by not using praise in their interactions with the toddlers. Previous studies (Maynard, 1999) have also shown older siblings lack of extrinsic verbal reinforcement such as praise. The tendency not to praise has also been seen in other East African communities such as the Gusii of Kenya where mothers rarely praised their infants and argued that praising children made them conceited and unwilling to take orders (Levine, 2002).

In addition, the fact that there were no gender differences suggests that although adult roles might be different, the socialization processes of everyday skills are still the same. The children in this study were involved in activities such as feeding animals, singing and dancing. These are activities that most children in rural Kenya engage in therefore this study informs us of the structures of the children's daily activities which are similar to those of the greater society.

The information on the children's interaction during daily activities therefore provides information about children's social organisation and also adds to our understanding of what children do when they are alone together and how they are internalising cultural modes for behaviour. In fact, the data has shown that the children's daily activities differed from those of the Zinacantec Maya children who taught their younger siblings how to wash baby dolls and cook tortillas. This is a clear indication that although children the world over may engage in play when they are alone together, the type of play or activities they engage in will differ from one culture to another.

This study also tells us of the structure of the children's social relationships which are a reflection of the society's hierarchical relationships for example, the older siblings were always in charge. These relationships exhibited in the children's play are therefore the foundation for later adult relationships. Therefore, as the siblings interacted, they were socializing each other to behave in culturally appropriate ways.

Although the older siblings may not always have requested the toddlers to pay attention or purposely engaged the toddlers in their activities, the toddlers were learning by observing their older siblings since children do learn through observation (Rogoff, et. al, 1993). Just by engaging in activities next to the toddlers and having the toddlers observe them, the older siblings in this study were being the mature members of the community who Tomasello et al. (1993) and Rogoff et al. (1993) argue have a central position as role models or instructors to younger members. The older siblings in this study were therefore cultural transmitters to the toddlers.

CHAPTER VI
CONCLUSION AND RECOMMENDATIONS

6.1 Conclusion

This study demonstrated that teaching, and not just learning, develops. The children in this study demonstrated teaching skills according to their age with older children displaying more advanced teaching skills. This implies that the children's teaching skills were developing as they got older.

This study also showed that children have the capability to use different teaching strategies which can either be verbal, non-verbal or both and that use of these strategies depends on the children's age with younger children using more nonverbal strategies while older children prefer verbal ones. Therefore, although children of different ages may have the ability to act as teachers to their younger siblings, the types of teaching strategies they employ will vary with age.

This study also demonstrated that teaching occurs in a cultural context. As they interacted, the children displayed social relationships which are a reflection of the wider Agikuyu society. They also demonstrated teaching skills according to their social status. The children's social organisation therefore reflected that of the greater Agikuyu society, and their hierarchical relationships were actually the foundation of later adult relationships. In addition, the daily activities that the children were engaged in such as feeding farm animals further showed that the Agikuyu children's daily activity structures are similar to those of adults. When compared to western or middle class societies this is a major difference as children's activities in western and middle class societies are segregated from those of adults. Therefore, when alone, Agikuyu children do engage in activities similar to those of adults. This study therefore demonstrates that children can be cultural transmitters to their younger siblings in Agikuyu society. The Agikuyu community is one that readily employs sibling caretaking especially when parents are engaged. This means that children can be important socialization tools to their younger siblings when left in charge of them. Agikuyu children can therefore be regarded as cultural teachers to their younger siblings.

6.2 Recommendations

In the following paragraphs some recommendations that can be derived from this study for the fields of application are articulated.

6.2.1 Parents

The children in this study taught their younger siblings how to sing, dance, feed animals and even play. These children therefore had an influence on their younger siblings and parents must therefore be aware of the role children can play as cultural transmitters of everyday activities. It appears that as children were being socialized by their parents, they were also socializing their younger siblings. Parents should therefore encourage and guide children to help their younger siblings.

The results of the study also showed that although the children may have engaged in positive behaviour such as offering help to the toddlers, there was also a tendency to direct negative behaviour towards them during the interactions. This is something that parents have to keep in mind since they have to realise that the probability of adverse episodes occurring during sibling interactions also exists. Much as they may encourage children to assist their younger siblings, they should also find ways to minimise the conflicts between siblings since negative behaviour from older siblings has been associated with younger siblings' poorer perceived self-competence and poorer adjustment (Cicirelli, 1994).

6.2.2 Educationalists

This study has shown how children teach their younger siblings and has therefore shown the possibility of siblings as guides for each others development. This means that if children are taught they can be teachers of each other, their skills can be used to help their younger siblings. This could perhaps even prove useful in the education sector for example in tutoring activities. Tutoring activities could be tailored so that children assist their younger siblings with their schoolwork and educationalists or teachers could inform parents of the possibility of encouraging children assist each other with homework.

6.3 Future studies

This study looked at children's teaching and involved children who were related. Future studies could possibly examine the differences between children's teaching with both related and unrelated toddlers. It would be interesting to find out what strategies children would use with unrelated toddlers as the possibility exists that children may use different strategies when teaching toddlers who are not related to them.

Sibling teaching in other cultures should also be explored for example in Europe, Asia or the United states in order to find out the sort of daily activities children in these cultures engage in. The children involved in this study engaged in activities that most children in Kenyan rural areas would engage in. It is possible that the daily activities of children in different cultures would be influenced by the cultural environment therefore it would also be interesting to see what sort of daily activities children in these other cultures engage in. These future studies of children's teaching in other cultures could also provide more information on the social and cognitive skills that children acquire over the course of middle childhood.

Comparative studies of sibling teaching by children from different communities in Kenya could also be done. The data in this study were obtained from the Agikuyu who are an Agrarian community. Future data could also be collected from Kenyan fishing, foraging or nomadic communities. The results of these studies could then be compared and an analysis made of the existing similarities and differences. A sample drawn from an urban area could also be used in future studies and the results compared to those of this study which had a sample from a rural area.

This study also only described and examined older siblings teaching but did not look at the toddlers' behaviour during the interactions. Future studies could therefore also examine the toddlers' behaviour during the interactions and perhaps also provide data as to whether the older siblings' teaching was effective.

6.4 Shortcomings and constraints of the study

Although most of the research process was smooth, there were however a few shortcomings and constraints of the study. During the data collection phase, some neighbour's children who did not realise that a videotaping session was going on wandered on to the scene and the research assistant had to call these children and send them on an errand to prevent them from interfering with the data collection process. The children did not understand why they were not to join the activities of the siblings who were being videotaped because on a normal day, children from different homesteads usually played together. Future studies should make provision for neighbours' children who wander on to the scene and their interactions with the toddlers could be compared to that of the older siblings' interactions with the toddlers as this is an even more natural environment for children's socialization.

Another shortcoming of this study was that some of the older siblings had small babies with them at the scene therefore did not direct all their attention to the toddlers. The reason there were babies at the scene is because in some homesteads there were no other individuals who could have watched over the babies during the videotaping sessions therefore the older siblings carried the babies to the scene. Perhaps future studies could plan for videotaping sessions only during the hours when most of the adults are in the homestead so that they can watch over the babies during the videotaping sessions. Another option would be to include the babies that is, not only observe the dyadic teaching but also analyse the complexity of the interactions as they occur.

Having the senior members of the households present may also be advantageous as they could also assist in controlling the activities of the visitors to the homesteads. Some of the visitors especially the elderly ones did not understand the importance of not talking loudly when the videotaping sessions were taking place nor did they understand why the researcher was hesitant to stop video recording and shake their hands in greeting. The research assistant did request all the adults present not to talk too loudly during the video recording sessions but some people forgot these instructions. Refusing to shake an elderly persons' hand in greeting or constantly correcting an elderly person is considered impolite among the Agikuyu therefore some interruptions due to these two activities did occur as the researchers sometimes had to shake hands in greeting since they did not want to offend the elderly people at the scene. During future studies however, the presence of senior members of the households could make the data collection process easier as these older individuals would assist in controlling the activities of visitors to the homesteads.

REFERENCES

Abramovitch, R., Corter, C., & Lando, B. (1979). Sibling interaction in the home. *Child Development, 50,* 997-1003.

Abramovitch, R., Corter, C., Pepler, D, & Stanhope, L. (1986). Sibling and peer interaction: A final follow-up and a comparison. *Child Development, 57,* 217-229.

Abravanel, E., & Gingold, H. (1985). Learning via observation during the second year of life. *Developmental Psychology, 21,* 614-623.

Ames, G. J., & Murray, F. B. (1982). When two wrongs make a right: Promoting cognitive change by social conflict. *Developmental Psychology, 18,* 894-897.

Azmitia, M., & Hesser, J. (1993). Why siblings are important agents of cognitive development: A comparison of siblings and peers. *Child Development, 64,* 430-444.

Bank, S. P., & Kahn, M. D. (1982). *The sibling bond.* New York: Basic Books, Inc.

Best, D. L., & Williams, J. E. (1997). Sex, gender and culture. In J. W. Berry, M. H. Segall & C. Kagitcibasi (Eds.), *Handbook of Cross-cultural Psychology, vol. 3: Social behaviour and applications* (2nd Ed.) (pp. 163-212). Boston: Allyn & Bacon.

Brazelton, T. B., Robey, J. S., & Collier, G. (1969). Infant development in the Zinacanteco Indians of Southern Mexico. *Pediatrics, 44,* 274-283.

Brody, G. H., Stoneman, Z., & MacKinnon, C. (1982). Role asymmetries in interactions between school-aged children, their younger siblings, and their friends. *Child Development, 53,* 1364-1370.

Brody, G. H., Stoneman, Z., MacKinnon, C. E., & MacKinnon, R. (1985). Role relationships and behaviors between preschool-aged and school-aged sibling pairs. *Developmental Psychology, 21,* 124- 129.

Brown, J. R., & Dunn, J. (1992). Talk with your mother or your sibling? Developmental changes in early family conversations about feelings. *Child Development, 63,* 336-349.

Buhrmester, D. (1992). The developmental courses of sibling and peer relationships. In F. Boer & J. Dunn (Eds.), *Children's sibling relationships: Developmental and clinical issues* (pp. 19-40). Hillsdale, NJ: Erlbaum.

Buhrmester, D., & Furman, W. (1990). Perceptions of sibling relationships during middle childhood and adolescence. *Child Development, 61,* 1387-1398.

Childs, C. P., & Greenfield, P. M. (1980). Informal modes of learning and teaching: The case of Zinacanteco weaving. In N. Warren (Ed.), *Studies in Cross-cultural Psychology* (Vol. 2, pp. 269-316). London: Academic Press.

Cicirelli, V. G. (1972a). The effect of sibling relationships on concept learning of young children taught by child teachers. *Child Development, 43,* 282-287.

Cicirelli, V. G. (1972b). Concept learning of young children as a function of sibling relationships to the teacher. *Child Development, 43,* 282- 287.

Cicirelli, V. G. (1973). Effects of sibling structure and interaction on children's categorization style. *Developmental Psychology, 9,* 132- 139.

Cicirelli, V. G. (1975). Effects of mother and older sibling on the problem-solving behaviour of the younger child. *Developmental Psychology, 11,* 749-756.

Cicirelli, V. G. (1976). Mother-child and sibling interactions on a problem-solving task. *Child Development, 47,* 588-596.

Cicirelli, V. G. (1994). Sibling relationships in cross-cultural perspective. *Journal of Marriage and the Family, 56,* 7-20.

Cicirelli, V. G. (1996). Sibling relationships in middle and old age. In G. H. Brody (Ed.), *Sibling relationships: Their causes and consequences* (pp. 47-73). Norwood, NJ: Ablex.

Conger, K. J., Conger, R. D., & Scaramella, L. V. (1997). Parents, siblings, psychological control and adolescent adjustment. *Journal of Adolescent Research, 12,* 113-138.

Counts, D. A. (1985). Sweeping men and harmless women: Responsibility and gender identity in later life. In J. Sokolovsky (Ed.), *Aging in the Third World: Part II* (pp. 1-26). Publication No. 23. Studies in Third World Societies. Williamsburg, VA: College of William and Mary.

Damon, W. (1980). Patterns of change in children's social reasoning: A two-year longitudinal study. *Child Development, 51,* 1010-1017.

Deater-Deckard, K., Dunn, J., & Lussier, G. (2002). Sibling relationships and social-emotional adjustment in different family contexts. *Social Development, 11,* 571-590.

Doise, W., & Mugny, G. (1979). Individual and collective conflicts of centrations in cognitive development. *European Journal of Psychology, 9,* 105-108.

Dunn, J. (1983). Sibling relationships in early childhood. *Child Development, 54,* 787-811.

Dunn, J. (1988). Annotation: Sibling influences on childhood development. *Journal of Child Psychology and Psychiatry, 29,* 119-127.

Dunn, J. (1996). Sibling relationships and perceived competence: Patterns of stability between childhood and early adolescence. In A. J. Sameroff & M. M. Haith (Eds.), *The five to seven shift: The age of reason and responsibility* (pp. 253-270). Chicago: University of Chicago Press.

Dunn, J. (2000). State of the art: Siblings. *Psychologist, 13,* 244-248.

Dunn, J., Brown, J., & Beardsall, L. (1991). Family talk about feeling states and children's later understanding of others' emotions. *Developmental Psychology, 27,* 448-455.

Dunn, J., Brown, J., Slomkowski, C., Tesla, C., & Youngblade, L. (1991). Young children's understanding of other people's feelings and beliefs: Individual differences and their antecedents. *Child Development, 62,* 1352-1366.

Dunn, J., & Dale, N. (1984). I a daddy: 2-year-olds' collaboration in joint pretend with sibling and with mother. In I. Bretherton. (Ed.), *Symbolic play* (pp. 131-158). New York: Academic Press.

Dunn, J., & Kendrick, C. (1982). *Siblings: Love, envy, and understanding.* Cambridge, MA: Harvard University Press.

Dunn, J., & Munn, P. (1985). Becoming a family member: Family conflict and the development of social understanding in the second year. *Child Development, 56,* 480-492.

Dunn, J., & Munn, P. (1986). Sibling quarrels and maternal intervention: Individual differences in understanding and aggression. *Journal of Child Psychology and Psychiatry, 27,* 583-595.

Dunn, J., & Munn, P. (1987). The development of justifications in disputes. *Developmental Psychology, 23,* 791-798.

Dunn, J., & Shatz, M. (1989). Becoming a conversationalist despite (or because of) having an older sibling. *Child Development, 60,* 399-410.

Eisenberg, A., & Garvey, C. (1981). Children's use of verbal strategies in resolving conflicts. *Discourse Processes, 4,* 149-170.

Estioko-Griffen, A., & Griffen, P. B. (1981). Woman the hunter: The Agta. In F. Dahlberg (Ed.), *Woman the gatherer* (pp. 121-152). New Haven, CT: Yale University Press.

Farver, J. (1993). Cultural differences in scaffolding pretend play: A comparison of American and Mexican mother-child and sibling-child pairs. In K. MacDonald, (Ed.), *Parent-child play: Descriptions and implications* (pp. 349-366). Albany, NY: SUNY Press.

Farver, J., & Howes, C. (1993). Cultural differences in American and Mexican mother-child pretend play. *Merrill-Palmer Quarterly, 39,* 344-358.

Farver, J. A. M., Kim, Y. K., & Lee, Y. (1995). Cultural differences in Korean and Anglo-American preschoolers' social interaction and play behaviors. *Child Development, 66,* 1088-1099.

Farver, J., & Wimbarti, S. (1995). Indonesian children's play with their mothers and older siblings. *Child Development, 66,* 1493-1503.

Felson, R. B. (1983). Aggression and violence between siblings. *Social Psychology Quarterly,* December.

Fortes, M. (1970). Social and psychological aspects of education in Taleland. In J. Middleton (Ed.), *From child to adult* (pp. 14-74). New York: National History Press. (Original work published 1938).

Freed, R. S., & Freed, S. A. (1981). *Enculturation and education in Shanti Nagar* (Anthropological Papers of the American Museum of Natural History, Vol. 57, Pt. 2). New York: American Museum of Natural History.

Freedman, D. G. (1979). Ethnic differences in babies. *Human Nature, 2,* 36-43.

Freedman, D. G., & Freedman, N. (1969). Behavioral differences between Chinese-American and European-American newborns. *Nature, 224,* 1227.

Furman, W., & Buhrmester, D. (1985a). Children's perceptions of the personal relationships in their social networks. *Developmental Psychology, 21,* 1016-1024.

Furman, W., & Buhrmester, D. (1985b). Children's perceptions of the qualities of sibling relationships. *Child Development, 56,* 448-461.

Garbarino, J. (1989). An ecological perspective on the role of play in child development. In M. N. Bloch & A. D. Pellegrini (Eds.), *The ecological context of children's play* (pp. 12-36). Norwood, NJ: Ablex Publishing Corporation.

Gaskins, S. (1990). *Exploratory play and development in Mayan infants.* Unpublished doctoral dissertation. University of Chicago.

Gaskins, S. (1999). Children's daily lives in a Mayan village: A case study of culturally constructed roles and activities. In A. Göncü (Ed.), *Children's engagement in the world: Sociocultural perspectives* (pp: 25-61). Cambridge: Cambridge University Press.

Gershaw, D. A. (1989). Birth order. *Line on life*. Retrieved March 8, 2004 from
http://www3.azwestern.edu/psy/dgershaw/lol/Birthorder.html

Glachan, N. M., & Light, P. H. (1982). Peer interaction and learning: Can two wrongs make a right? In G. E. Butterworth & P. H. Light (Eds.), *Social cognition: Studies in the development of understanding* (pp.238-262). Chicago: University of Chicago Press.

Göncü, A., Mistry, J., & Mosier, C. (2000). Cultural variations in the play of toddlers. *International Journal of Behavioral Development, 24,* 321-329.

Goodale, S. (1971). *Tiwi wives*. Seattle: University of Washington Press.

Goodluck, H. (1991). *Language acquisition: A linguistic introduction.* Oxford, U.K.: Blackwell.

Gopnik, A., & Meltzoff, A. N. (1994). Minds, bodies, and persons: Young children's understanding of the self and others as reflected in imitation and theory of mind research. In S. T. Parker & R. W. Mitchell (Eds.), *Self-awareness in humans and animals: Developmental perspectives* (pp. 166-186). Cambridge, U.K.: Cambridge University Press.

Goudena, P. P. (1987). The social nature of private speech of preschoolers during problem solving. *International Journal of Behavioral Development, 10,* 187-206.

Greenfield, P. M. (1972). Studies of mother-infant interaction: Toward a structural-functional approach. *Human Development, 15,* 131-138.

Greenfield, P. M. (1984). A theory of the teacher in the learning activities of everyday life. In B. Rogoff & J. Lave (Eds.), *Everyday cognition: Its development in social context* (pp. 117-138). Cambridge, MA: Harvard University Press.

Greenfield, P. M. (1994). Independence and interdependence as developmental scripts: Implications for theory, research, and practice. In P. M. Greenfield & R. R. Cocking (Eds.), *Cross- cultural roots of minority child development* (pp. 1-37). Hillsdale, NJ: Lawrence Erlbaum.

Greenfield, P. M. (2002). The mutual definition of culture and biology in development. In H. Keller, Y. H. Poortinga & A. Schölmerich (Eds.), *Between Culture and Biology*. Cambridge: Cambridge University Press.

Greenfield, P. M., Brazelton, T. B., & Childs, C. (1989). From birth to maturity in Zinacantan: Ontogenesis in cultural context. In V. Bricker & G. Gossen (Eds.), *Ethnographic encounters in Southern Mesoamerica: Celebrating essays in honor of Evon Z. Vogt* (pp. 177-216). Albany: Institute of Mesoamerican Studies, State University of New York.

Greenfield, P. M., Keller, H., Fulgni, A., & Maynard, A. (2003). Cultural pathways through universal development. *Annual Review of Psychology, 54,* 461-490.

Greenfield, P. M., & Lave, J. (1982). Cognitive aspects of informal education. In D. Wagner & H. Stevenson (Eds.), *Cultural perspectives on child development* (pp. 181-207). San Francisco: Freeman.

Greenfield, P. M., & Suzuki, L. (1998). Culture and human development: Implications for parenting, education, pediatrics, and mental health. In I. E. Sigel & K. A. Renninger (Eds.), *Handbook of child psychology: Vol. 4. Child psychology in practice* (5th ed., pp. 1059-1109). New York: Wiley.

Gregory, E. (2002, June). Sibling support. *Literacy today, 31.* Retrieved March 22, 2004, from
http://www.literacytrust.org.uk/Pubs/gregory.html.

Greitemeyer, T., Rudolph, U., & Weiner, B. (2003). Whom would you rather help: An acquaintance not responsible for her plight or a responsible sibling? *Journal of Social Psychology, 143*, 331-340.

Haight, W., & Miller, P. (1993). *Pretending at home: Early development in sociocultural context*. Albany: SUNY Press.

Hancock, T. B., & Kaiser, A. P. (1996). Siblings' use of milieu teaching at home. *Topics in Early Childhood Special Education, 16*, 168-190.

Harkness, S., & Super, C. M. (1986). The cultural structuring of children's play in a rural African community. In K. Blanchard (Ed.), *The many faces of play* (pp. 96-103). Champaign, IL: Human Kinetics.

Harkness, S., & Super, C. (1995). Culture and parenting. In M. H. Bornstein (Ed.), *Handbook of parenting, vol. 2: Biology and ecology of parenting* (pp. 211-234). New Jersey, UK: Lawrence Erlbaum Associates, Publishers.

Harkness, S., & Super, C. M. (2002). The ties that bind: Social networks of men and women in a Kipsigis community of Kenya. *Ethos, 29*, 357-370.

Harter, S. (1983). Developmental perspectives on the self-system. In E. M. Hetherington (Eds.), P. H. Mussen (Series Ed.), *Handbook of child psychology: Vol. 4. Socialization, personality, and social development* (pp. 275-385). NY: Wiley.

Haviland, L. K. M. (1978). *The social relations of work in a peasant community*. Unpublished doctoral dissertation, Harvard University, Cambridge, MA.

Hewlett, B. S. (1988). Sexual selection and parental investment among Aka pygmies. In L. Betzig, M. Borgerhoff-Mulder & P. Turke (Eds.), *Human reproductive behaviour: A Darwinian perspective* (pp. 263-276). Cambridge, England: Cambridge University Press.

Hewlett, B. S., & Cavalli Sforza, L. L. (1988). Cultural transmission among Aka pygmies. *American Anthropologist, 88*, 922-934.

Hewlett, B. S., de Silvertri, A., & Guglielmino, C. R. (2002). Semes and genes in Africa. *Current Anthropology, 43*, 305-335.

Hewlett, B. S., & Lamb, M. E. (2002). Integrating evolution, culture and developmental psychology: Explaining caregiver infant proximity and responsiveness in Central Africa and the United States of America. In H. Keller, Y. H. Poortinga & A. Schölmerich (Eds.), *Between Culture and Biology: Perspectives on ontogenetic development* (pp.241-269). New York: Cambridge University Press.

Hoff-Ginsberg, E., & Krueger, W. (1991). Older siblings as conversational partners. *Merrill-Palmer Quarterly, 37*, 465-481.

Howe, N. (1991). Sibling-directed internal state language, perspective taking, and affective behaviour. *Child Development, 62*, 1503-1512.

Howe, N., Rinaldi, C. M., Jennings, M., & Petrakos, H. (2002). "No! The lambs can stay out because they got cozies": Constructive and destructive sibling conflict, pretend play, and social understanding. *Child Development, 73*, 1460-1473.

Howe, N., & Ross, H. S. (1990). Socialization, perspective-taking, and the sibling relationship. *Developmental Psychology, 26*, 160-165.

Ivey, P. K. (1992). The Efe forager infant and toddler's pattern of social relationships: Multiple and simultaneous. *Developmental Psychology, 28*, 568-577.

Jahoda, G. (1982). *Psychology and anthropology: A psychological perspective*. New York: Academic Press.

Kagitcibasi, C. (1996). *Family and human development across cultures: A view from the other side*. Mahwah, NJ: Lawrence Erlbaum.

Katz, L. F., Kramer, L., & Gottman, J. M. (1992). Conflict and emotions in marital, sibling, and peer relationships. In C. U. Chantz & W. W. Hartup, (Eds.), *Conflict in child and adolescent development* (pp. 122-149). Cambridge: Cambridge University Press.

Keller, H. (2000). Developmental Psychology I: Prenatal to Adolescence. In K. Pawlik & M. R. Rosenzweig (Eds.), *International Handbook of Psychology* (pp. 235-260). London: Sage.

Keller, H. (2002). Culture and Development: Developmental Pathways to Individualism and Interrelatedness In W. J. Lonner, D. L. Dinnel, S. A. Hayes & D. N. Sattler (Eds.), *OnLine Readings in Psychology and Culture* (Unit 11, Chapter 1), (http://www.wwu.edu/~culture), Department of Psychology, Center for Cross-Cultural Research, Western Washington University, Bellingham, Washington USA:

Keller, H., & Eckensberger, L. H. (1998). Kultur und Entwicklung (Culture and development). In H. Keller (Ed.), *Lehrbuch Entwicklungspsychologie* (pp. 57-96). Bern, Switzerland: Huber Verlag.

Keller, H., & Greenfield, P. M. (2000). History and future of development in cross-cultural psychology. In C. Kagitcibasi & Y. H. Poortinga (Eds.), *Millenium Special Issue of the "Journal of Cross Cultural Psychology"*, 31, 52-62.

Kenya Ministry of Finance and Planning (2002). *Thika District Development Plan 2002-2008*. Nairobi: Rural Planning Department Ministry of Finance and Planning Republic of Kenya.

Kenyatta, J. (1965). *Facing Mt. Kenya*. USA: Random House Inc.

Klein, P. S., Feldman, R., & Zarur, S. (2002). Mediation in a sibling context: The relations of older siblings' mediating behaviour and younger siblings' task performance. *Infant and Child Development, 11*, 321-333.

Klein, P. S., Zarur, S., Feldman, R. (2003). Mediational behaviours of preschoolers teaching their younger siblings. *Infant and Child Development, 12*, 233-242.

Koinange, J. W. (2001, Summer). Psychology strides forward in Kenya. *Psychology International, 12*, 3.

Konner, N. (1976). Maternal care, infant behavior and development among the !Kung. In R. B. Lee & I. DeVore (Eds.), *Kalahari hunter gatherers of the !Kung San and their neighbours* (pp.218-245). Cambridge, MA: Harvard University Press.

Kontos, S. (1983). Adult-child interaction and the origins of metacognition. *Journal of Educational Research, 77*, 43-54.

Kruger, A. C., & Tomasello, M. (1986). Transactive discussions with peers and adults. *Developmental Psychology, 22*, 681-685.

Levine, R. A. (2002). Challenging expert knowledge: Findings from an African study of infant care and development. In U. P. Gielen & J. L. Roopnarine (Eds.), *Childhood and Adolescence in Cross-cultural Perspectives*. Forthcoming.

Levine, R. A., Dixon, S., Levine, S., Richman, A., Leiderman, P. H., Keefer, C. H., & Brazelton, T. B. (1994). *Child care and culture: Lessons from Africa*. New York, NY: Cambridge University Press.

Lollis, S., Van Engen, G., Burns, L., Nowack, K., & Ross, H. (1999). Sibling socialization of moral orientation: "Share with me!" "No, it's mine!" *Journal of Moral Education, 28*, 339-357.

MacDonald, K., & Parke, R. D. (1984). Bridging the gap: Parent-child play interaction and peer interactive competence. *Child Development, 55*, 1265-1277.

Malley, C. (1991). *Toddler development*. Amherst, MA: University of Massachusetts.

Markus, H. R., & Kitayama, S. (1991). Culture and the self: Implications for cognition, emotion, and motivation. *Psychological Review, 98*, 224-253.

Masur, E., & Ritz, E. (1984). Patterns of gestural, vocal, and verbal imitation performance in infancy. *Merrill-Palmer Quarterly, 30*, 369-392.

Matsumoto, D., Kudoh, T., & Takeuchi, S. (1996). Changing patterns of individualist and collectivist in the United States and Japan. *Culture and Psychology, 2*, 77-107.

Maynard, A. E. (1999). Cultural teaching: *The social organization and development of teaching in Zinacantec Maya sibling interactions.* Unpublished doctoral dissertation, University of California, Los Angeles.

Maynard, A. E., & Greenfield, P. M. (2003). Cultural teaching and learning: Processes, effects, and development of apprenticeship skills. In Z. Bekerman (Ed.), *Learning in places: The informal education reader.* New York: Counterpoints.

McCall, R., Parke, R., & Kavanaugh, R. (1977). Imitation of live and televised models by children one to three years of age. *Monographs of the Society for Research in Child Development, 42,* Serial No. 173.

McGillicuddy-De Lisi, A. V. (1993). Sibling interactions and children's communicative competency. *Journal of Applied Developmental Psychology, 14,* 365-383.

McGuire, S., Manke, B., Eftekhari, A., & Dunn, J. (2000). Children's perceptions of sibling conflict during middle childhood: Issues and sibling (dis)similarity. *Social Development, 9,* 173-190.

Mead, M. (1953). *Growing up in New Guinea.* New York: Mentor Books

Meisner, J. S., & Fisher, V. L. (1980). Cognitive shifts of young children as a function of peer interaction and sibling status. *The Journal of Genetic Psychology, 136,* 247-253.

Meltzoff, A. N. (1988a). Infant imitation and memory: Nine-month-olds in immediate and deferred tests. *Child Development, 59,* 217-225.

Meltzoff, A. N. (1988b). Infant imitation after a one week delay: Long term memory for novel acts and multiple stimuli. *Developmental Psychology, 24,* 470-476.

Mendelson, M. J., Villa, E. P. de, Fitch, T. A., & Goodman, F. G. (1997). Adults' expectations for children's sibling roles. *International Journal of Behavioral Development, 20,* 549-572.

Middleton, J. (Ed.). (1970). *From child to adult: Studies in the anthropology of education.* New York: National History Press.

Minnett, A. M, Vandell, D. L., & Santrock, J. W. (1983). The effects of sibling status on sibling interaction: Influence of birth order, age spacing, sex of child, and sex of sibling. *Child Development, 54,* 1064-1072.

Morelli, G., Rogoff, B., & Angelillo, C. (submitted). Cultural variation in young children's access to work or involvement in specialized child-focused activities.

Mugny, G., & Doise, W. (1978). Sociocognitive conflict and the structure of individual and collective performance. *European Journal of Social Psychology, 8,* 181-192.

Munroe, R. H., & Munroe, R. L. (1971). Household density and infant care in an East African society. *Journal of Social Psychology, 83,* 3-13.

Munroe, R. H., Munroe, R. L., Michelson, C., Koel, A., Bolton, R., & Bolton, C. (1983). Time allocation in four societies. *Ethnology, 22,* 355-370.

Munroe, R., Munroe, R., & Shimmin, H. (1984). Children's work in four cultures: Determinants and consequences. *American Anthropologist, 86,* 369-377.

National Academy of Sciences (1994). *Cultural Diversity and Early Education: Report of a Workshop.* Washington, D. C.: National Academy Press.

Newman, J. (1996). The more the merrier? Effects of family size and sibling spacing on sibling relationships. *Child: Care, Health and Development, 22,* 285-302.

Nie, N. H., Stein, B. K., & Bent, D. H. (1975). *SPSS - Statistical Package for the Social Sciences* (2nd ed.) New York: McGraw-Hill.

Nuckolls, C. (1993). *Siblings in South Asia.* New York: Guilford Press.

Parmar, P., Harkness, S, & Super, C. M. (2004). Asian and Euro-American parents' ethnotheories of play and learning: Effects on preschool children's home routines and school behaviour. *International Journal of Behavioural Development, 28,* 97-104.

Pepler, D. J., Abramovitch, R., & Corter, C. (1981). Sibling interaction in the home: A longitudinal study. *Child Development, 52,* 1344-1347.

Pepler, D. J., Corter, C., & Abramovitch, R. (1983). Social relations among children: Comparison of sibling and peer interaction. In K. Rubin & H. Ross (Eds.), *Peer relationships and social skills in childhood.* New York: Springer-Verlag.

Perlman, M., & Ross, H. S. (1997). The benefits of parent intervention in children's disputes: An examination of concurrent changes in children's fighting styles. *Child Development, 64,* 690-700.

Phinney, J. S. (1986). The structure of 5-year-old's verbal quarrels with peers and siblings. *The Journal of Genetic Psychology, 147,* 47-60.

Piaget, J. (1952). *The origins of intelligence in children.* New York: International Universities Press.

Piaget, J. (1967). *Six psychological studies.* Toronto, Ontario, Canada: Randon House.

Prochaska, J. M., & Prochaska, J. O. (1985). Children's views of the causes and cures of sibling rivalry, *Child Welfare, 64,* 427-433.

Provisional census results show Kenya population stands at 28 million. (2000, February 28). *The Daily Nation.*

Rabain-Jamin, J., Maynard, A. E., & Greenfield, P. M. (2003). Implications of sibling caregiving for sibling relations and teaching interactions in two cultures, *Ethos, 31,* 1-28.

Radcliffe-Brown, A. R. (1964). *The Adaman islanders.* New York: Free Press of Glencoe. (Original work published 1932).

Ratner, H., & Hill, L. (1991). *Regulation and representation in the development of children's memory.* Paper presented to the Society for Research in Child Development, Seattle, WA.

Rindstedt, C. (2001). *Quichua children and language shift in an Adean community: School, play and sibling caretaking.* Unpublished doctoral thesis, The Tema Institute, Department of Child Studies, Linköping University, Linköping, Sweden.

Rogoff, B. (1986). Adult assistance of children's learning. In T. E. Raphael (Ed.), *The contexts of school based literacy* (pp. 27-40). New York: Random.

Rogoff, B. (1990). *Apprenticeship in Thinking: Cognitive development in social context*. Oxford University Press: New York.

Rogoff, B. (2003). *The cultural nature of human development*. New York: Oxford University Press.

Rogoff, B., Mistry, J., Göncü, A., & Mosier, C. (1993). Guided participation in cultural activity by toddlers and caregivers. *Monographs of the Society for Research in Child Development, Serial No. 236, Vol. 58(8)*.

Rogoff, B., Sellers, M. J., Pirotta, S., Fox, N., & White, S. H. (1975). Age of assignment of roles and responsibilities to children: A cross-cultural survey. *Human Development, 18*, 353-369.

Romeo, F. F. (1994). A child's birth order: Educational implications. *Journal of Instructional Psychology, 21*, 155-161.

Roopnarine, J. L., Hooper, F. H., Ahmeduzzaman, M., & Pollack, B. (1993). Gentle play partners: Mother-child and father-child play in New Delhi, India. In K. Macdonald (Ed.), *Parent-child: Descriptions and implications* (pp. 287-304). Albany, NY: SUNY Press.

Ross, H., Martin, J., Perlman, M., Smith, M., Blackmore, E., & Hunter, J. (1996). Autonomy and authority in the resolution of sibling disputes. In M. Killen (Ed.), *Children's autonomy, social competence, and interactions with adults and other children: Exploring connections and consequences: Vol. 73. New Directions for Child Development* (pp. 71-90). San Francisco: Jossey-Bass.

Ross, H. S., Filyer, R. E., Lollis, S. P., Perlman, M., & Martin, J. L. (1994). Administering justice in the family. *Journal of Family Psychology, 8*, 254-273.

Ruble, D. N., Boggiano, A. K., Feldman, N. S., & Loebl, J. H. (1980). Developmental analysis of the role of social comparison in self-evaluation. *Developmental Psychology, 16*, 105-115.

Ruddle, K., & Chesterfield, R. (1978). Traditional skill training and labor in rural societies. *Journal of Developing Areas, 12,* 389-398.

Santrock, J. W. (2001). *Child development* (9th ed.). Boston: McGraw-Hill.

Schwartzman, H. B. (1986). A cross-cultural perspective on child-structured play activities and materials. In A. W. Gottfried & C. C. Brown (Eds.), *Play interactions. The contribution of play materials and parental involvement to children's development.* Lexington, MA: D.C. Heath and Company.

Sharma, V. P. (1996). Older siblings can become bossy. Retrieved March 9, 2004, from http:77www.mindpub.com/art333.htm

Steinmetz, S. K. (1977). The use of force for resolving family conflict: The training ground for abuse. *The Family Coordinator, 26,* 19-26.

Stewart, R. B. (1983). Sibling interaction: The role of the older child as teacher for the younger. *Merrill-Palmer Quarterly, 29,* 47-68.

Stoneman, Z., & Brody, G. H. (1993). Sibling temperaments, conflict, warmth, and role asymmetry. *Child Development, 64,* 1786-1800.

Stoneman, Z., Brody, G. H., & MacKinnon, C. E. (1986). Same-sex and cross-sex siblings: Activity choices, roles, behaviour, and gender stereotypes. *Sex Roles, 15,* 495-511.

Straus, M., Gelles, R., & Steinmetz, S. (1980). *Behind closed doors.* New York: Doubleday.

Tomasello, M. (1992). *First verbs: A case study in early grammatical development.* Cambridge: Cambridge University Press.

Tomasello, M., Conti-Ramsden G., & Ewert, B. (1990). Young children's conversations with their mothers and fathers: Differences in breakdown and repair. *Journal of Child Language, 17,* 115-130.

Tomasello, M., Kruger, A. C., & Ratner, H. H. (1993). Cultural learning. *Behavioral and Brain Sciences, 16,* 495-552.

Tomasello, M., & Mannle, S. (1985). Pragmatics of sibling speech to one year olds. *Child Development, 56,* 911-917.

Trevarthen, C., & Logotheti, K. (1989). Child and culture: Genesis of co-operative knowing. In A. Gellatly, D. Rogers & J. A. Sloboda (Eds.), *Cognition and social worlds* (pp.37-56). Oxford, U.K.: Clarendon Press/Oxford University Press.

Triandis, H. C. (1995). *Individualism and Collectivism.* Boulder, CO: Westview Press.

Tronick, E. Z., Morelli, G. A., & Ivey, P. K. (1992). The Efe forager and toddler's pattern of social relationships: Multiple and simultaneous. *Developmental Psychology, 28,* 568-577.

Tucker, C. J., Barber, B. L., & Eccles, J. S. (1997). Advice about life plans and personal problems in late adolescent sibling relationships. *Journal of Youth and Adolescence, 26,* 63-76.

Van Volkom, M. (2003). The relationships between childhood tomboyism, siblings' activities, and adult gender roles. *Sex Roles, 49,* 609-618.

Vandell, D. L, & Bailey, M. D. (1992). Conflicts between siblings. In C. U. Shantz & W. W. Hartup (Eds.), *Conflict in child and adolescent development* (pp. 242-269). New York: Cambridge University Press.

Vandermass-Peler, M. (2002). Cultural variations in parental support of children's play. In W. J. Lonner, D. L. Dinnel, S. A. Hayes & D. N. Sattler (Eds.), *Online Readings in Psychology and Culture* (Unit 11, Chapter 3), (http://www.www.edu/~culture), Center for Cross-Cultural Research, Western Washington University, Bellingham, Washington USA.

Verhoef, H., & Morelli, G. A. "Please don't interrupt me, I'm talking": Cultural variation in toddlers' attention-seeking efforts and caregivers' responses. (Submitted to International Journal of Behavioral Development).

Volk, D. (1999). "The teaching and the enjoyment and being together": Sibling teaching in the family of a Puerto Rican kindergartner. *Early Childhood Research Quarterly, 14,* 5-34.

Volling, B. L. (2003). Sibling relationships. In M. H. Bornstein, L. Davidson, C. L. M. Keyes, K. A. Moore & the Center for Child Well-being (Eds.), *Well-being: Positive development across the life course* (pp. 205-220). Mahwah, NJ: Erlbaum.

Vygotsky, L. S. (1967). Play and its role in the mental development of the child. *Soviet Psychology, 5,* 6-18.

Vygotsky, L. S. (1978). *Mind in society: The development of higher mental processes.* Cambridge, MA: Harvard University Press.

Vygotsky, L. S. (1990). Imagination and creativity in childhood. *Soviet Psychology, 28,* 84-96.

Watson-Gegeo, K. A., & Gegeo, D. W. (1989). The role of sibling interaction in child socialization. In P. G. Zukow (Ed.), *Sibling interaction across cultures: Theoretical and methodological issues* (pp. 54-76). New York: Springer-Verlag.

Weisner, T. S. (1982). Sibling interdependence and child caretaking: A cross-cultural view. In M. E. Lamb & B. Sutton-Smith (Eds.), *Sibling relationships: Their nature and significance across the lifespan* (pp. 305-327). Hillsdale, NJ: Lawrence Erlbaum.

Weisner, T. S. (1989). Cultural and universal aspects of social support for children: Evidence from the Abaluyia of Kenya. In D. Belle (Ed.), *Children's social networks and social supports* (pp. 70-90). New York: Wiley Interscience.

Weisner, T. S., & Gallimore, R. (1977). My brother's keeper: Child and sibling caretaking. *Current Anthropology, 18,* 169-190.

Wenger, M. (1989). Work, play, and social relationships among children in a Giriama community. In D. Belle (Ed.), *Children's social networks and social supports* (pp. 91-115). New York: Wiley Interscience.

West, S. A., Pen, I., & Ashleigh, S, G. (2002). Cooperation and competition between relatives. *Psychology and Behavioural Sciences Collection, 296,* 72-75.

Whaley, S. E., Sigman, M., Beckwith, L., Cohen, S. E., & Espinosa, M. P. (2002). Infant-caregiver interaction in Kenya and the United States: The importance of multiple caregivers and adequate comparison samples. *Journal of Cross-cultural Psychology, 33*, 237-247.

Whiting, B. B., & Edwards, C. P. (1988). *Children of different worlds: The formation of social behavior.* Cambridge, MA: Harvard University Press.

Whittemore, R. D., & Beverly, E. (1989). Trust in the Mandika: The cultural context of sibling care. In P. G. Zukow (Ed.), *Sibling interaction across cultures: Theoretical and methodological issues* (pp. 26-53). New York: Springer-Verlag.

Wimmer, H., & Perner, J. (1983). Beliefs about beliefs: Representation and constraining function of wrong beliefs in young children's understanding of deception. *Cognition, 13*, 103-128.

Wood, D., Bruner, J., & Ross, G. (1976). The role of tutoring in problem-solving. *Journal of Child Psychology and Psychiatry, 17*, 89-100.

Yeh, H., & Lempers, J. D. (2004). Perceived sibling relationships and adolescent development. *Journal of Youth and Adolescence, 33*, 133-147.

Yewchuk, C. R., & Schlosser, G. A. (1996). Childhood sibling relationships of eminent Canadian women. *Roeper Review, 18*, 287-292.

Youngblade, L. M., & Dunn, J. (1995). Individual differences in young children's pretend play with mother and sibling: Links to relationships and understanding of other people's feeling and beliefs. *Child Development, 6*, 1472-1492.

Zukow, P. G. (1989). Siblings as effective socializing agents: Evidence from Central Mexico. In P. G. Zukow (Ed.), *Sibling interaction across cultures. Theoretical and methodological issues* (pp. 79-105). New York: Springer-Verlag.

Zukow-Goldring, P. (1995). Sibling caregiving. In M. H. Bornstein (Ed.), *Handbook of parenting, vol. 3: Status and social conditions of parenting* (pp. 179-208). Hillsdale, NJ, Lawrence Erlbaum Associates, Inc.

APPENDIX 1
INTERVIEW SCHEDULE FOR TODDLERS' MOTHERS

1. Name of the Researcher:
2. Date:
3. District:
4. Division:
5. Subject code:

Background Information on the Toddler

6. Name of the toddler:
7. Date of birth of the toddler:
8. Sex of the toddler:
9. Name of the mother:
10. Mothers' marital status:
11. Date of birth
    (a) Mother:
    (b) Father:
12. Occupation
    (a) Mother:
    (b) Father:
13. Highest level of education attained
    (a) Mother:
    (b) Father:
14. Birth position of the toddler:
15. Number of toddlers' older siblings:
16. Older siblings dates of birth and gender

Date of birth	Gender
1.	
2.	
3.	
4.	
5.	

17. (a) Do all the above siblings live in the same homestead as the toddler?
    Yes or No:
17. (b) If no, which of these siblings live outside the homestead and where?

17. (c) Why do they live outside the homestead?

18. Who else lives in the homestead apart from the toddlers' older siblings?

Individual (relation to the toddler)	Gender	Age
1.		
2.		
3.		
4.		
5.		
6.		
7.		

Activities during Caretaking of the Toddler

19. Apart from yourself, who else normally takes care of the toddler?
20. What activities do each of these individuals perform with the toddler when caretaking?

Person	Relationship	Activities
1.		
2.		
3.		

Mothers' opinion

21. What do you understand by the term teaching?
22. When should children start being taught?
    Why?

CURRICULUM VITAE

EDUCATION

1979 - 1986	Primary school in Thika, Kenya at Gatumaini primary school
1987 - 1990	High school in Nairobi, Kenya at The Kenya High School
1992 - 1996	Undergraduate studies in Nairobi, Kenya at Kenyatta University Bachelor of Education
1997 - 2000	Postgraduate studies in Nairobi, Kenya at Kenyatta University Master of Education
April, 2002 - January 2005	Doctoral studies in Osnabrück, Germany at Universität Osnabrück PhD (Developmental Psychology)

WORK EXPERIENCE

November 1997 - October 2001	Graduate Assistant in the Educational Psychology Department of Kenyatta University, Nairobi
November 2001 - March 2005	Tutorial Fellow in the Educational Psychology Department of Kenyatta University, Nairobi

www.ingramcontent.com/pod-product-compliance
Lightning Source LLC
Chambersburg PA
CBHW030828230426
43667CB00008B/1436